LEFT
FOR
DEAD

A YOUNG MAN'S SEARCH FOR JUSTICE
FOR THE USS *INDIANAPOLIS*

LEFT
FOR
DEAD

PETE NELSON

with a preface by HUNTER SCOTT

DELACORTE PRESS

Published by
Delacorte Press
an imprint of Random House Children's Books
a division of Random House, Inc.
1540 Broadway
New York, New York 10036

Visit us on the Web!
www.randomhouse.com/teens

Educators and librarians, for a variety of teaching tools, visit us at
www.randomhouse.com/teachers

Library of Congress Cataloging-in-Publication Data

Nelson, Peter.
Left for dead : a young man's search for justice for the USS Indianapolis / Peter
Nelson ; with a preface by Hunter Scott.
p. cm.
Summary: Recalls the sinking of the U.S.S. Indianapolis at the end of World War II, the
navy cover-up and unfair court martial of the ship's captain, and how a young boy
helped the survivors set the record straight fifty-five years later.
ISBN: 0-385-72959-6 (trade)—ISBN: 0-385-90033-3 (GLB)
1. Indianapolis (Cruiser)—Juvenile literature. 2. McVay, Charles Butler, d. 1968—
Trials, litigation, etc.—Juvenile literature. 3. Scott, Hunter, 1985–—Juvenile literature.
4. Trials (Naval offenses)—United States—Juvenile literature. 5. World War,
1939–1945—Naval operations, American—Juvenile literature. [1. Indianapolis
(Cruiser) 2. McVay, Charles Butler, d. 1968—Trials, litigation, etc. 3. Scott, Hunter,
1985– 4. Trials (Naval offenses) 5. World War, 1939–1945—Naval operations,
American.] I. Title.

D774.I5 N35 2002
940.54'5973—dc21

2001053774

The text of this book is set in 11-point Transit 551BT.

Book design by Kenny Holcomb

Manufactured in the United States of America

May 2002

10 9 8 7 6 5 4 3 2

BVG

To the final crew of the USS *Indianapolis* (CA-35)

–Pete Nelson

LEFT
FOR
DEAD

Contents

Preface

I was standing in front of my history fair project, surrounded by a cluster of men in their mid-seventies and -eighties. Their families, children and grandchildren were also gathered around. These men had one thing in common: They were all survivors of the USS *Indianapolis*. I had developed a special appreciation for these men and what they had done in World War II. I had learned to appreciate these veterans who had sacrificed so much to ensure that a generation that had not been alive when they served could enjoy liberty.

It was July 1997, and we were in the Westin Hotel in Indianapolis. The second floor was crammed with men, women and children of all ages. There were display cases lined up along the walls, all pertaining to World War II or the *Indianapolis*. Everywhere I went, I was surrounded by ten or twenty men. They all had communicated with me in some fashion over the course of the past year, and each wanted to personally tell me his story of his four nights and five days in the ocean. To a man, when their story reached a point at which they talked about shipmates and friends dying, their eyes teared up, and I could sense the deep sadness and the emotional scars each of them carried.

Maybe that is why so few of them had ever shared their personal stories and dark memories until I started asking questions. Many of these men had never told their family members what they shared with me. I am not sure why I was chosen to be the guardian of their stories, but I accepted the task with the same honor and commitment these men had shown in sharing their tales with me. Perhaps they thought I might represent their last chance to tell someone what had been haunting them for more than fifty years. Each man I talked to thanked me for what I was doing for them and their captain.

Let me tell you a little bit about what got me involved with the survivors of the USS *Indianapolis*. My name is Hunter Scott. I am sixteen years old and in the eleventh grade at Pensacola High School. For the past two years I was elected class president and Young Republicans president, and I am an active athlete as well. I am the center on the football team and a pole-vaulter on the track team. I attend First Baptist Church of Pensacola and am the lead guitarist in the church's youth band and a sax player in the worship band. Playing my guitars and hunting, fishing and surfing are some of my favorite activities.

When I was eleven years old, in the summer of 1996, I was getting ready to enter middle school and the sixth grade. On an afternoon that was unusually hot even for Florida, my dad and I were watching his favorite movie, *Jaws*. In one part of the movie, Captain Quint and the other two guys have had a little too much to drink and are telling stories about how tough they are. One guy asks Captain Quint what that tattoo is on his arm. Quint tells the story of the *Indianapolis*. As I listened to the story of men being attacked by sharks, I was fascinated. I had heard what Quint said before, but this was the first time I had really listened.

When the scene was over, I stood up and asked my dad if it was a true story. My dad said, "Yes, and please move from in front of the TV." I asked him again to tell me more about it. He said he didn't know much about the incident other than that it was a true story. Being a school principal, he gave an answer I should have expected: "If you want to know more, I will take you to the library and you can check out a book on the USS *Indianapolis*."

I was looking for a topic for a history fair project, and after hearing the story of the ship, I knew I had my subject. The theme for that year was "Triumph and Tragedy," and this story had both. Little did I know that what started as a simple history project would consume the next five years of my life and provide an experience very few are ever afforded. Nor did I realize that this project would allow me to work with some of the most powerful people in Washington, D.C., and would embroil me in a legal battle with one of the oldest and most prestigious institutions in America, the United States Navy.

My dad was doing research for his dissertation that summer and decided to take me to the University of West Florida's library to teach me how to do research. I must admit, a fishing trip with Dad would have been my first preference, but dads love teaching certain life lessons to their sons, and that day's life lesson happened to be research. On our first trip he took me down to the World War II section of the library. He pulled out a large stack of books, placed them on the table, showed me how to use an index and set a legal pad on the table. He told me he was going upstairs and would be back in one hour. I was to write on the legal pad summaries of what I found and where, and when he returned we would discuss what I had discovered.

When he got back he looked disappointed to see only four or five lines written on my legal pad. He gave me a solemn look and I heard a familiar question: "What have you been doing for the last hour?" I told him there was almost nothing in any of the books about the USS *Indianapolis*. I could tell he was a little skeptical about my answer. With an "I will show you how to do this" look, he sat down with the books himself.

In the end he told me there was something wrong. He wanted to know why the greatest sea disaster in naval history was not thoroughly discussed in the history books. He took me upstairs and showed me how to do a microfiche search of 1945 newspapers. We found some information about the USS *Indianapolis* and the court-martial of Captain McVay, who was blamed for the sinking, but still very few facts. An Internet search also provided little useful information. Why was the greatest naval wartime loss of life not thoroughly discussed in detail in history books, in old newspapers or on the Internet?

My history teacher had told me that interviews with individuals who had lived through historical events were a primary resource and very valuable. I decided to try to locate survivors of the *Indianapolis*. My mom suggested putting an ad in the *Gosport*, a local navy newspaper, requesting information about the *Indianapolis* and survivors. A response to the ad helped me locate survivor Maurice Glenn Bell, who lived in Mobile, Alabama. I called and set up an interview in his home.

Mr. Bell was a wonderful man, and his story was even more chilling than the scene in *Jaws*. I felt a lot of compassion for Mr. Bell after all he had been through. He believed that Captain McVay had been done an injustice. After I interviewed Mr. Bell, my project became a mission. I decided to try to right a wrong that had been done more than fifty years before. Mr. Bell showed me his Purple Heart, told me about his job as a lookout on the ship, and explained how his faith in God had helped him survive the ordeal. He also gave me a USS *Indianapolis* hat. Most importantly, he gave me a list of the remaining survivors. Of the 317 men who survived the sinking, 154 were still alive. In 1996 these men ranged in age from sixty-nine to ninety-two.

I started by writing to forty of the survivors whose names I recognized from the sources I had read, asking for additional information. The response was tremendous. Many of these men sent personal memorabilia, pictures, letters and original navy documents. Many survivors decided for the first time in their lives to write about what had happened to them during their five days and four nights surrounded by sharks and death.

Many of these men had never told their own children what they told me. I am not sure why they trusted me with their stories of terror and of the deaths of friends. Some of the material the survivors sent was so graphic that my dad, unknown to me, decided not to let me read it. Later he said he was not sure that a boy of eleven could comprehend what men will do to survive or was capable of understanding what these men had gone through, or of understanding the horrors of war.

I also interviewed Morgan Moseley, another survivor. Mr. Moseley too believed that Captain McVay should not have been court-martialed. Mr. Moseley was the ship's cook. He had been sick and had not eaten for two days when he entered the water. He told me he had lost forty-five pounds while floating in the sea. He said in a life-or-death situation, a person's mental and spiritual condition determines whether he will survive.

These men and their testimony helped me become even more committed to helping restore the reputation of their captain and honor their own heroism.

My dad says all young people need dream builders in their lives. He says that too many students are surrounded by dream destroyers. Dream destroyers are people who will tell you all the reasons you can't do something instead of helping you build your dreams. I have learned never to let anyone destroy my dreams.

In 1997, with the conviction that I could make a difference, I wrote to President Clinton and John Dalton, then Secretary of the Navy, and asked for the court-martial to be reopened or for the President to pardon Captain McVay. Both of their offices responded with very nice but stern "no" letters. I think one wonderful thing about being eleven years old is that a letter from the office of the President or the Secretary of the Navy saying something cannot be done doesn't mean too much. At least, those letters did not mean much to me.

If the President and the Secretary of the Navy would not help me, I decided, I would accomplish my goal by winning the State and National History Fair. That would ensure that my project would be displayed in Washington and would bring national attention to the cause of the survivors of the USS *Indianapolis*. I won the school and county competition in the spring of 1997. I was the only sixth grader ever to win the county competition, and my project was judged one of the best ever.

To get ready for the state competition, I sent a questionnaire to the remaining 114 survivors. Again the response was tremendous. All these men believed their captain had been made a scapegoat. Many filled out the questionnaire and also called to tell me their stories. Some of these conversations are burned indelibly in my memory. I remember survivor Herbert J. Minor telling me about holding up one of his friends in the water: "I was trying to hold his head out of the water but he kept slipping. . . . I yelled at everyone near me to help for a moment, but no one even looked up. I could feel him bump my feet on the way down." Survivor Sam Lopetz recalled, "There were two hundred thirty or more men in our group. Only sixteen survived the ordeal on the cargo nets." Survivor Paul J. Murphy said, "Fear was beyond words. Especially when a shark swam between your legs."

I could not forget these stories. None of us should forget what these men did for us. A naval historian looked at my collection of information on the *Indianapolis* and told me that my project was becoming one of the greatest collections of information on this topic in the world.

I was extremely excited at the state history fair competition, held on the campus of Florida State University in Tallahassee. My project drew large crowds. When I went for my interview, the three judges would not even let me tell them about my project. I was so upset that I started to cry. My dad came out of the bleachers because he could tell something was wrong. We went outside and I told him what had happened.

After the judging we went back inside and saw a large easel with a page of the history fair rules enlarged and highlighted in front of my project. The page contained a footnote: "Notebooks are not to be displayed with the project." I had been disqualified for displaying notebooks with the survivors' interviews and personal memorabilia. But I had been instructed to display the notebooks by our county history fair coordinator because of the historical significance of the documents in the notebooks.

I was heartbroken. Then my dad reminded me of one of his favorite sayings—"The true test of a man's character is what it takes to make him quit"—and asked me what I would do next. Sometimes dads say the right thing at the right time. I needed a dream builder at that moment, and my dad was one. I felt I had let the men of the *Indianapolis* down. I dreaded the thought of calling the men who had put so much trust in me and telling them I had failed. I made the calls and the men were very supportive, but I could not shake the feeling that this could not end now.

Congressman Joe Scarborough heard what had happened to me at the state history fair and asked whether my project could be displayed in his Pensacola office. Pensacola being a navy town, word of my project spread, and people lined up in Congressman Scarborough's office to look at my project and read my interviews with the survivors. The local paper covered the story; it was carried over the Associated Press wire and attracted Tom Brokaw's attention. Mr. Brokaw wanted to feature me on *NBC Nightly News*.

In July 1997, I was invited to be the guest of honor at the *Indianapolis* survivors' reunion in Indianapolis. I was allowed to ride in the first fire truck in the survivors' parade. I gave speeches at each assembly and said the opening prayer at the prayer service, and I was the only nonsurvivor allowed to walk in with the survivors at the memorial service and lay a flower at the base of the memorial. I felt as if I were surrounded by grandfathers.

At the reunion I met one of Captain McVay's sons, Charles McVay IV. He was moved by what I was doing for his father and said he and the survivors had tried for years to vindicate his father, with no success. Like any son, he was proud of his dad and still angry at the way the navy had treated him.

The national media covered the survivors' reunion, and Tom Brokaw showcased my mission on the "American Spirit" segment of *NBC Nightly News*. One thing about trying to change something through legislation: Media attention helps a lot. I have learned that the media will listen to a serious twelve-year-old. One reporter asked me an interesting question: "If you do a school history project and end up changing history, how do you grade something like that?" I had never thought about my project in that way before. Over the next couple of years, I would learn just how hard it is to change history.

Kimo McVay, the second of Captain McVay's sons, saw me on *Prime Time Country* and *NBC Nightly News* and contacted me. Kimo could not believe what I had done and what I was trying to do for his father and the survivors of the USS *Indianapolis*. The McVay family and the survivors had tried for more than fifty years to correct this injustice and had gotten nowhere, and in a short period I had brought the matter to the attention of the nation and appeared to be on the way to rewriting history.

Kimo wanted me to visit him in Hawaii, and I was also invited to take a ride on the nuclear submarine USS *Indianapolis* by the skipper, Commander Bill Toti. My family decided that a trip to Hawaii would be nice, and we went to meet Kimo and take Commander Toti up on his offer. Kimo gave me many papers and other items that had belonged to his dad. He also gave me his father's dog tags from the naval academy, as well as a lighter that was given to his dad at the first survivors' reunion in 1960. I also received a plaque given to Kimo when the *Indianapolis* memorial was dedicated in 1990, since his dad was no longer alive by then. These are the most precious items in my *Indianapolis* collection. They make me feel closer to Captain McVay. It is a strange feeling to feel close to someone you have never met. Kimo said his father was looking down on me and saying, "Well done, young man."

My research had convinced Congressman Scarborough that an injustice had been done to Captain McVay, and he drafted legislation to clear the captain's name. In January 1998, I met another dream builder, Mike Monroney, once a very powerful and prominent lobbyist in Washington. Mr. Monroney read about me and decided to come out of retirement to help with this legislation. He might have sailed on the *Indianapolis*'s last voyage, but an illness had kept him onshore. The thought that he might have been aboard had haunted him for more than fifty years. Mr. Monroney became the driving force behind the Washington legislative effort, pouring enormous energy and passion into the process.

Our trip to Washington to introduce the bill was set for April 1998. The bill was written, and Congresswoman Julia Carson from Indianapolis agreed to co-introduce it. Congressman Scarborough, Congresswoman Carson and Mike Monroney got appointments for me to meet with many congresspeople and senators and with Speaker of the House Newt Gingrich.

The media attention surrounding my trip to Washington was enormous. I was on all the morning shows: *Good Morning America,* NBC's *Today* and *CBS This Morning.* I also received coverage on the nightly news shows on ABC, NBC, CBS, Fox and CNN and did radio interviews that were broadcast on NPR across the United States as well as in France, England, Ireland, Germany and Canada. The story was carried on the front page of *The New York Times* and *USA Today.* My mission was also written about in eighteen other countries, including Japan. The entire world was becoming informed about the USS *Indianapolis.*

On the day the bill was to be introduced, I spoke at a press conference in Washington with Congressman Scarborough, Congresswoman Carson and fifteen survivors of the *Indianapolis.* I had never seen so many camera crews in my life. I counted at least twenty crews and more reporters than that, with their cassette recorders and notepads. As the bill and my mission to correct an injustice gained momentum, people from all over the world who had bits and pieces of the story found a way to contact me and provide me with more information. I even received at my school packages addressed to "Hunter Scott, Pensacola, Florida."

As this information came in, I began to build an even stronger case that the navy had used Captain McVay as a scapegoat to cover its mistakes. I developed a portfolio of proof that I distributed to members of the House and Senate. When you're twelve, it's important to have all the facts when you meet with members of Congress. Because of my age, I was granted access to some of the most influential politicians in Washington. I was told that no representative or senator likes to be seen on camera saying no to a young boy. At a party after the legislation had been introduced, the USS *Indianapolis* Survivors Organization made me an honorary member. This was an honor that I greatly appreciated. My heroes were honoring me, when it is they who are the true heroes.

For the next year everyone involved worked hard to get legislation passed that would clear Captain McVay's name. We got further along in the 106th congressional session than we had been at the end of the 105th session. Now legislation had been introduced in both the House and the Senate. The legislation would express the "sense of Congress" that Captain McVay's court-martial had been a miscarriage of justice and never should have happened. It would also award a Presidential Unit Citation to the USS *Indianapolis*'s final crew, in recognition of their courage in the face of tremendous hardship.

On September 14, 1999, at the age of fourteen, I testified along with several survivors before the Senate Armed Services Committee. The head of the committee, Senator John Warner, informed me that I was the youngest witness ever to appear before the committee. Senator Warner had said he was going to gavel the hearing in and stay for about fifteen minutes, and then he would have to leave. Once the hearing officially began, we stayed before the committee for more than three hours and won over Senator Warner, who remained through the entire hearing. Senator Warner said that he had come to the hearing fully ready to support the navy's position but had "righted his course" after listening to our testimony. It seemed we were winning the battle.

The past five years of my life have been a journey down a bumpy road with many jolts and upsets, but well worth every bump. My dad says you learn more about an individual's character after a defeat than after a win. I have learned that winners shake off the bumps, don't cast blame or make excuses, and continue down the road with their goals and destination intact.

This journey I have made has allowed me to learn the true cost of freedom. Throughout America's history, men and women have put their lives on the line, while losing friends and loved ones, to ensure that you and I and all Americans can enjoy liberty. Through my fight to exonerate the captain of the USS *Indianapolis,* I am trying to pay back at least a little bit of honor to some of the people who provided my freedom. I am trying to honor a group of veterans to whom honor is everything.

Hunter Scott
Pensacola, Florida

Chapter One

The Sailor
July 1945

The horror has seared my mind like a hot poker and I cannot forget it. After fifty years the dates and faces have lost their distinction, but the horror never gives way. The older I get, the more it bothers me. I can still hear the screams of the injured and dying.

Cozell Smith, 1994

The sailor finds himself swimming in the open ocean, wondering in shock how it came to this so suddenly. It's just past midnight. He'd been sleeping above deck, because it was too hot below and it smelled of sweat and bad breath and dirty laundry. He woke up at eleven-thirty, half an hour before his turn to stand watch. He went to the mess hall, grabbed a cup of coffee from the fifty-gallon urn and took his coffee topside. A quarter moon appeared briefly in a break in the clouds, high overhead. Now it's dark. He looks up, straining to see the moon. There's no light. The last light he saw was his ship on fire, flames, smoke, mixed with the horrible sounds of men screaming.

1

"I can't swim!" the man hanging on to him shouts.

The sailor wonders how they could let a man who can't swim join the navy. The sailor's name is Cozell Lee Smith, but they call him Smitty. The man whose life he's saving is named Dronet. Smith has no life jacket. Dronet has no life jacket. Smith has already warned Dronet not to get scared and grab him around the neck, that he'll leave him if he does. He'll save Dronet's life if he can, but if he has to, he will cut him loose. He's already tiring. He's a strong swimmer, but Dronet is heavy, weighing him down.

Smith swims. He gets a mouthful of seawater. He spits, coughs, keeps swimming. He inhales fumes and feels sickened by them. He hears screaming. He wonders how many others there are. He can't see a thing. It's too dark. He can't tell what direction the screaming is coming from. He strains for breath and accidentally swallows another mouthful of seawater, but it's not just seawater. It's fuel oil from the ship's ruptured tanks, thick and gooey. Instantly he's covered in it. It goes down his throat. More fumes. He feels sick and retches. He pushes his vomit away from him in the water. Dronet is coughing.

"What is it?" Dronet asks.

"Oil," Smith gasps. "Hang on. Keep kicking."

The irony is that if Smith hadn't joined the navy, he might well have been working in the oil fields back in Oklahoma. He'd volunteered at the age of seventeen, fresh out of tenth grade. His father, a barber, signed the permission papers with the thought that joining the navy might keep his son out of the kind of trouble a boy might get into, hanging around in a small town with nothing to do.

He spits. The oil goes down his throat even when he tries not to swallow. The ship burned oil to heat its boilers, which created the steam needed to turn the turbines to drive the propellers, which seamen call screws. It was, for its size, one of the fastest ships in the world, with a flank speed of thirty-two knots. He'd been standing at his watch station in "the bathtub," an antiaircraft battery protected by a circular splinter shield, shooting the breeze with Jimmy Reid, another coxswain from his division, when they heard the explosion. The shock of the blast nearly knocked him off his feet.

"What the heck was that?" Smith asked. Reid said he thought it was a boiler exploding.

"That could be good," Reid said. Smith wondered what could be good about it. "We'll go back to the States for repair," Reid explained.

Then the ship began to list, still moving forward but tilting to starboard, five degrees, then ten. Smith thought it would stop any second, but it didn't, listing fifteen degrees, then twenty. It slowly dawned on him that the unthinkable was coming to pass. They were sinking. Were they? Impossible. Not impossible—it was happening. When the list reached thirty degrees, he climbed down from his position and scrambled to the high side, grabbing hold of the steel cable lifeline that girded the ship. Other men had nothing to grab on to and fell. One man fell backward into the number three gun turret and hit it hard with his head. His head cracked with a sound like Babe Ruth hitting a baseball. That man was dead. A second man fell into the gun turret, and Smith could hear his bones break. The ship kept rolling over on its side until it reached ninety degrees. Smith ran across the hull of the overturned ship. In the dim light, through the smoke, he saw other men scattered down the length of the ship, some running, some standing frozen with fear. He was about to jump off the keel when Dronet stopped him and asked him for help, explaining that he couldn't swim. Now they're together in the water.

A scream. Smith looks around. Where is the screaming coming from? Is a scream something to be avoided or approached? He swims. Smith is tired. His eyes sting from the oil. He looks up. The moon is again breaking through the clouds. He tries not to swallow salt water.

"Kick!" Smith commands.

The screams grow louder. They swim to a group of men, about eight in all.

"Oh God, oh God, oh God," one is screaming. "Let me go. Just let me go, please. . . ."

"Hang on."

"No—let me go. . . ."

"Hang on!"

Two men are supporting the man who's screaming. The screaming man has his arms around the shoulders of the other two. His eyes open and close. His mouth is open in a grimace. Smith notices something white, shining in the waxing moonlight. It's the man's bones. The flesh has burned off his arms and his bones are showing. The salt water stings him. He wants to die. He wants the others to let him die but they won't. Smith says nothing. The man with the burned arms looks around, looks at Smith, then looks away. He's in agony. The others speak to him, urging him to hold on. Then his head tilts forward, face in the water. For a long time, he doesn't move. The two men supporting the man with the burned arms finally give him up for dead and release him. The man whose bones are showing floats toward Smith and Dronet. Smith is exhausted from supporting Dronet and feels as if he's about to drown. The man whose bones are showing is wearing a life jacket he doesn't need anymore, so Smith takes it off him and helps Dronet into it. Dronet can't swim—he needs the life jacket more than Smith does. Freed from the jacket, the burned man sinks.

For now there's enough buoyancy in the life jacket to support both of them. Smith finally rests, hanging on to his new friend.

In the distance he hears somebody shouting, "Help me—somebody! Please! Oh God . . ." Other men scream but don't use words. Men are injured. Men are dying all around him. There is confusion everywhere. Smith tries not to panic. He can't help anybody right now. Two men near him in the water are talking.

"Torpedoes," one says.

"How many?"

"I heard three."

The moon disappears. When it's gone, it's pitch-black. The screams continue through the night, men suffering from and succumbing to their injuries. As the screams abate, Smith realizes the quiet doesn't mean things are getting better—it means only that men who were screaming have died. He feels lucky that he has no injuries, but that isn't much to feel lucky about.

At first light, the seas are calm. Smith is cold and welcomes the light because he knows it will bring warmth. He's covered in oil, thick and greasy. It stings his eyes. Dronet is covered in oil too. Everyone is, shiny black unidentifiable faces bobbing in the water. As the light grows in strength, he sees something floating in the water near him. Hanging on to Dronet, he kicks toward it, hoping it's food or water, but instead it's a body. He can't tell whose.

There were 250 new recruits on the ship. They were all headed for the Philippines for gunnery practice, before an invasion of the Japanese main islands. What sense did that make? Smith had been firing the guns for over two years—he didn't need any practice. The dead man is floating facedown. Smith swims away from the body. He looks around. He sees a second body, then a third. There are bodies everywhere. *How many of my shipmates are dead? How many of us have survived?* He sees a splash in the distance, and thinks it could be a man slapping his hand against the water, trying to swim, but then he sees a fin. The terror of it hits him. To his left he watches as a body is suddenly pulled under. He sees a tail.

The water is full of sharks.

Chapter Two

The Boy
November 1996

Futile the winds
To a heart in port, —
Done with the compass,
Done with the chart.

Emily Dickinson

An old man sits in his leather-upholstered recliner with his hands folded calmly in his lap. His house, in Mobile, Alabama, is a comfortable ranch on a dead-end street. The old man was once a sailor and still owns a small boat, but it's been a while since he's taken it out. It's the winding down time in his life, when the pull of the future begins to lose its power. In old age, memories merge and meld, or break loose and drift away. Things that happened fifty years ago seem like they happened only yesterday, while things that actually happened only yesterday slip the mind and disappear.

A boy kneels on the floor in front of the old man. He is here for the old man's memories. His name is Hunter Scott, and he is eleven years old. He's working on a project for his school's history fair. The theme of the fair this year is "Triumph and Tragedy." The boy wants to know about the war.

The old man's name is Maurice Glenn Bell, and he is seventy-one years old, born February 17, 1925, the same year Adolf Hitler published *Mein Kampf* and John Scopes went on trial in Tennessee for teaching evolution. Bell regards the young man. He has spoken to schoolchildren before, but he's never had one approach him with such keenness. The boy is wearing sneakers, jeans, a navy blue windbreaker over a white turtleneck. He has a sweet face and an easy smile, large brown eyes with long lashes. Some boys his age are already trying to cultivate an edge, but Hunter isn't interested in that. He has driven with his family from nearby Pensacola, Florida, a military town where at the highway rest areas, old jet fighters propped on pylons point defiantly toward the sky. Hunter's voice has a soft twang to it, his speech punctuated with the "yes, sirs" and "no, ma'ams" one hears from Southern kids taught to be polite and to respect their elders. He holds the old man's Purple Heart in his hands, and understands that it's a medal given to men who were wounded in action, but he doesn't really know what that means. His first question is, "What do they put on it to make it purple?"

Bell says he isn't sure. He considers. There are reasons for old men to tell young boys about war, and there are reasons not to. Some men feel it's too easy to tell a war story, too simple to catch a young man's interest with tales of high risk or near-death experiences, and too inadequate to leave it at that, out of context. You don't want to make something horrible sound appealing. Some feel there's no way to ever put it all into words, so why try? If you don't want to lie about it, but you can't really tell the truth either, silence becomes the only alternative. Men who survive know that the difference between those who make it home and those who get left behind is more a matter of fate than merit, and nothing to take any personal credit for. Generally speaking, the men of Bell's generation who served in World War II didn't talk much about the war afterward. Nonetheless, Maurice Bell invites Hunter to ask any questions he wants, and promises he'll do his best to answer them.

"How long did you serve on the *Indianapolis* and what were your duties?" the boy asks, reading from a set of questions he's prepared.

"I served two years on the *Indy*," Bell says in a firm sure voice. He speaks slowly, softly. "I did boot camp at Great Lakes, Illinois. I was in the Seventh Division. We were charged with cleaning the decks and manning the twenty-millimeter antiaircraft guns, so I guess I helped shoot down some planes. Some Japanese planes."

It's the first time Hunter has talked to a WWII veteran. It reminds him of a scene in a movie, which was how he got involved in this history fair project in the first place. The movie was Steven Spielberg's *Jaws*, about a massive great white shark menacing the waters of a summer resort island. The scene was the one where police chief Brody (played by Roy Scheider), marine biologist Hooper (Richard Dreyfuss) and Captain Quint (Robert Shaw) wait through the night aboard Quint's fishing boat for the harpooned killer shark to surface. They pass a bottle around, swapping scar stories and sea chanteys until Hooper asks Quint about the place on his arm where he's had a tattoo removed.

"*Don't tell me,*" Hooper says, laughing hysterically, " '*Mom . . .*' "

"*That, Mr. Hooper, was the USS* Indianapolis," Quint says ominously. Quint's fictional account is historically inaccurate. He gets the dates wrong. It's also highly dubious that any survivor of the *Indy* would ever have a tattoo of the ship removed. The men who served on the *Indianapolis* loved their ship, despite what happened to it, or maybe because of what happened to it.

"*You were on the Indianapolis?*" Hooper asks.

9

"What happened?" Brody wants to know.

"Japanese submarine slammed two torpedoes into our side, Chief," Quint says. *"It was comin' back from the island of Tinian Delady, just delivered the bomb. The Hiroshima bomb. Eleven hundred men went into the water. Vessel went down in twelve minutes . . ."*

It was while watching *Jaws* with his dad that Hunter got the idea for his history project. Triumph and Tragedy. Captain Quint was a fictitious character, an invention of author Peter Benchley. Maurice Bell had actually been there.

"Did you know what your mission was or what the cargo was that you were carrying?" Hunter asks Bell, reading from his clipboard.

"No, we didn't," Bell says. "I helped load and unload it but they didn't tell us what it was. We welded some containers to the deck so they wouldn't move but we didn't know what was in 'em." He remembers the rumors, that the crates were full of scented toilet paper being shipped to General MacArthur, supreme commander of the southwest Pacific theater and hero of the Philippines.

"Do you remember what you were doing when the torpedoes hit?" Hunter asks.

"That was my night to sleep all night," Bell answers. "Usually we had to stand watch part of every night, but every fourth night you were allowed to sleep the whole night. My first thought was that one of the boilers had exploded. That's what I thought. It was dark and then the emergency lights came on, and I reached for my life jacket but I couldn't find one, so I went up on deck to get one, and then when I found one, just as I reached my hand down to get it, somebody snatched it away." Bell leans over the side of his recliner and reaches his hand to the floor to illustrate. Hunter tries to imagine what Bell must have felt when the life preserver was suddenly gone. Bell remembers how they were supposed to keep their life preservers with them, how they'd taken on a fresh shipment of them in San Francisco just before sailing. After he grabbed another life preserver, his memory goes blank.

"You know, I've tried my best all these years to remember what happened next," Bell continues, "but it all was happening pretty fast. One of the torpedoes blew the bow off, but the ship was still moving at sixteen or seventeen knots, so the force of the water coming in crushed the bulkheads. Bulkhead after bulkhead. I grabbed hold of one of the lifelines and the next thing I remember, I was standing on one of the ship's screws, about forty feet up in the air, and I jumped from there. My feet were on the side of the ship and it rolled on over as I was jumping. The first thing I was afraid of was the suction from the ship sinking. And after that I was afraid the Japanese sub that sank us was going to come back and strafe the survivors, because I'd heard they did that."

Hunter tries to imagine what it would be like to be in the middle of the ocean, swimming for your life. His father, Alan Scott, an educator, worked on fishing boats as a kid and was once a semiprofessional sports fisherman. Hunter has hauled in blacktip sharks off the pier and duskies off the beach, practicing "catch and release" now that the shark populations have been decimated by overfishing. Hunter isn't afraid of sharks, but that's easy to say when you're standing safely on a beach or boat. In the movie *Jaws*, Quint's soliloquy about sharks was more frightening than anything Steven Spielberg did with screaming actors or animatronic fish, words that conjured up feelings of hopelessness and terror.

"Didn't see the first shark for about a half an hour," Quint tells Brody and Hooper. *"Tiger. Thirteen-footer. You know how you know that when you're in the water, Chief? You tell by lookin' from the dorsal to the tail. Well, what we didn't know, 'cause our bomb mission had been so secret—no distress signal had been sent. They didn't even list us overdue for a week. Very first light, Chief, the sharks come cruisin', so we formed ourselves into tight groups. You know, it's kinda like the old squares in battle, like you see on a calendar, like the battle of Waterloo. And the idea was, the*

shark would go for the nearest man and then he'd start poundin' and hollerin' and screamin' and sometimes the shark would go away. Sometimes he wouldn't go away. Sometimes that shark, he looks right into you. Right into your eyes. You know the thing about a shark, he's got . . . lifeless eyes, black eyes, like a doll's eye. When he comes at ya, doesn't seem to be livin'. Until he bites ya and those black eyes roll over white . . ."

After hearing Quint's monologue, Hunter had stood up, blocking the television, and asked his dad, "Was that true?" His father suggested he move aside. Then the middle school principal in him replied, "Well, why don't you go to a library and find some books and look it up?" It was Hunter's history teacher, Mrs. Prevatte, who suggested he interview sources in person for his history fair project. Hunter placed an advertisement in the *Gosport,* a navy newspaper out of the naval air station in Pensacola. In the ad, Hunter introduced himself as a sixth grader at Ransom Middle School, looking for survivors of the *Indianapolis*. Maurice Bell answered the ad.

"The man next to me when I jumped had been taking a shower when the torpedoes hit, so he was completely naked," Bell remembers. The naked man had held on to Bell until he could find a life jacket of his own.

"I wound up in one of the largest groups," Bell continues. "We had three rafts, so we put the men who were wounded in the rafts. I remember one man had broken his back, so we put him in the raft. We had no water. Somebody found a can of malted milk balls. Just enough to make me hungry. The seas weren't so bad that night. There were no breakers, you see—just big rollers, so you don't really know how rough it is. We really couldn't tell."

"Did you see people get attacked by sharks?" Hunter asks.

Bell has lived with this for over fifty years. He has answered this question before.

"I saw several," he says. "One man in particular comes to mind.

He'd drifted off maybe fifteen or twenty feet from me, and it seemed like everything had gotten real quiet, and then he screamed as the shark attacked, and all of a sudden he went straight down. And I never saw him again. The shark must have grabbed him by the leg or something. What happened was that two or three other sharks would see the water splashing, and then they'd come in and try to get him."

Hunter tries to imagine what it would feel like to know that at any second, you could be pulled out of the world you know, gone in the blink of an eye.

"That was how it was. Everything would get real quiet, and then all of a sudden the sharks would start attacking. They would go in a circle around us, and then that circle would get smaller and smaller."

The old man stirs the air in front of him to demonstrate, making broad sweeping circles with two fingers pointing down. Hunter has seen circling sharks in cartoons. He wonders how a man could have stood five minutes of this, let alone the five nights and four days the men of the *Indianapolis* spent in the water.

"Then," Bell says, his hands in front of him, palms facing down, fingers together, thumbs extended, "they would come right in and start attacking us." He pushes his hands forward and down until the thumbnails touch. "All over. Sometimes they'd come up from the bottom, or from the sides. I knew I could have been grabbed at any time, but by the grace of the Lord they didn't."

"Did you have any fears?" Hunter asks, wide-eyed.

"Well, I didn't know," Bell says, "but I never gave up. If I had, I wouldn't be here. One man we found floating with his head down, with his face towards the water, and I held him up for three or four hours, but finally he gave up and died. I took his life jacket off him, and we took the stuff from his pockets and put it in the raft, you know, to send to his family or whatever, and then we let him go. But I never thought I was going to die, so I just never gave up. A lot of 'em just died from the exposure. They'd just give up, or else they'd have hallucinations. I almost did. One time some guys I was with started saying they saw an island over there, saying, 'Look at all the beautiful girls in grass skirts with baskets of fruit on their heads,' and the girls were singin' and hollerin' and offerin' us glasses of fruit juice. I looked and looked and I almost saw 'em, two or three times, but I never did see 'em. But I come close. We had a little bit of rain one day, but just enough to get a few drops on my tongue. The thing was that the water down by our feet was cold all the time, even though the water up by our heads would get pretty warm during the day, so guys would dive down to get a drink because they thought the cold water down by their feet was fresh water. A few hours later, they'd be dead too. The water was so salty it'd swell your throat up and cut you off. I probably would have drunk it too but I wasn't that out of my head yet. I guess my biggest fear then was that they weren't going to find us, because planes would fly over, sometimes two a day, and we'd try to signal 'em but they'd just keep on going. Finally a plane come down, but it had its torpedo doors open, so we thought maybe they thought we were the enemy. The pilot was a man named Wilbur Gwinn, and he spotted us. They say he was fixing his antenna and that's what made him look out and see us."

It was dark, entering into the fifth night, before Maurice Bell was rescued. Bell recalls other planes arriving on the scene once Gwinn sounded the alarm, ships as well, and how the fear then was that somehow they'd be missed or overlooked and left behind.

"One of the men in our group," Bell tells the boy, "had a small flashlight that we were supposed to be able to use to signal SOS, but we'd been trying it for days and it didn't work. Well, one of the men in the small boat that picked us up said he thought he saw the light flicker for just a second." Bell isn't sure what to make of this, but allows for the possibility of divine intervention, an angel in a flashlight.

"And they came over and got us. I was covered in black fuel oil, but fortunately I didn't get any of it in my eyes like some of the others had. They'd put men in metal stretchers and then when the waves would rise up, the sailors on board the bigger ship would grab hold of it. And when I got on board I tried to take one step and started falling forward, and two other sailors grabbed me just before I hit the deck. I might not have survived that fall. Then a big old sailor sat me down on a bucket in the shower and started scrubbing, trying to get the oil off my head, but I kept sliding off the bucket so he got in the shower with me and held me up. They cut my clothes off me and gave me clean underwear and then they took me to the cafeteria and gave me some food, and I looked at it and said, 'I can eat more'n that,' so he said, 'You can eat all you want,' but two bites made me sick. They gave me a glass of water or juice and put me to bed and I just slept, and when I woke up I turned over and saw a sailor and he offered me a cold glass of milk, and it was the best milk I ever had in my life."

Bell was brought to a hospital in Guam. He was there when the war ended.

"By then," he tells the boy, "I was in the main part of the hospital and able to get up and walk around. I'm glad they dropped the bomb. I know it killed a lot of Japanese people, but we were preparing for the invasion of Japan and it would have killed millions on both sides if we did."

When Hunter asks him whom he blames for the tragedy, Bell answers first that he doesn't blame the Japanese submarine captain, a man named Mochitsura Hashimoto. "The Japanese were out to sink all the ships they could, just like the navy was trying to sink all the Japanese ships they could," he says. "Hashimoto was only doing his duty to his country."

The men of the *Indianapolis* were proud to have helped deliver the weapon that ended the war, honored to have been chosen for the task and for the role they played in history, just as they were proud of their ship and of their captain, a man named Charles Butler McVay III. When Hunter asks him whom he blames for the tragedy, Bell thinks of how the navy treated his captain after the war ended. Bell is proud of his country, proud of the cause and the mission he participated in as a young man, so long ago. Maurice Bell had a harder time being proud of the navy in which he served after it court-martialed Captain McVay, the only captain to be tried out of the approximately 350 captains who lost their ships during the war.

"That was the worst thing the navy could have done," the old man tells the boy. A palpable sadness enters his voice. "It dishonored the captain and the crew. I'll never sail again, but if I did, I would want Captain McVay as my captain, because he was one of the finest men I've ever met. I went to New Orleans once and looked him up and visited with him after the war. He was at the first reunion we had, in 1960, but he wasn't at the next one because his doctors wouldn't let him come."

When Hunter had first begun researching the sinking of the *Indianapolis,* after seeing *Jaws,* he'd found that most of the accounts of the war in the Pacific treated the incident as a footnote. Finally he tracked down a book called *Fatal Voyage* by Dan Kurzman, which told the full story of the sinking and its aftermath. What had happened to Captain McVay, Hunter came to discover, was as shocking as what had happened to his men in the water.

McVay had been afraid to come to the first survivors' reunion, fearful that his men still blamed him for what happened to them. Before July 29, 1945, he'd been a perfect captain, popular and respected, commanding but approachable, quite handsome with black eyebrows and graying hair that gave him a Cary Grant–like dignity. To his men, he seemed confident and capable but not aloof or detached, no by-the-books Naval Academy drone. He was a sportsman who'd occasionally taken time, when the war allowed it, to shoot skeet off the fantail, or throw a fishing line over the side, sometimes inviting his men to join him. He didn't undermine his own authority by fraternizing with his men, but he didn't overexert his authority over them either.

Captain McVay was a ladies' man who'd supposedly dated Hollywood starlets. He'd married a Hawaiian heiress named Kinau and had two sons by her, Charles IV and Kimo, before marrying his second wife, Louise. His father was an admiral, as was his grandfather. It was entirely expected in the McVay family that Charles number three would someday himself achieve the rank of admiral, if not Fleet Admiral or chief of the navy.

In some ways, Hunter Scott can identify with Captain McVay. He's been hunting since he was five and knows a thing or two about shotguns, and he loves to fish. As the son of a middle school principal, Hunter can appreciate what it's like to have for a father an authority figure who expects a lot of his son. Hunter can imagine the shame Captain McVay must have felt at his court-martial, knowing that his father was looking on.

What Hunter cannot imagine, because he's only eleven and because no one can truly know the heart and soul of someone in deepest despair, is what must have been going through the captain's mind when, at the age of seventy, on a cold November day in 1968, he lay down in the front yard outside his house in Litchfield, Connecticut, and shot himself through the head with his navy-issued .38-caliber revolver. Hunter can't understand either why relatives of the men who died on the *Indianapolis* sent Captain McVay hate mail for the rest of his life, hounding him long after the fact, particularly during the holidays. Surely Captain McVay felt responsible, even if losing the ship wasn't his fault. Surely he grieved the loss of his crew. Surely he empathized with the wives and parents and families they left behind. Why were they trying to make it worse? Is that the reason, Hunter wonders, why he was holding a small toy sailor when he killed himself?

Why did the navy blame him?

It took the *Indianapolis* only fourteen minutes to sink. It took her captain twenty-three years and three months to follow her down. He left no suicide note. No one will ever know exactly what he was thinking when he pulled the trigger. Hunter knows only that there is something confusing that needs to be clarified, and something wrong that needs to be corrected. The captain's name should be cleared, not just for the captain's sake, but for the sake of men like Maurice Bell. Captain Charles Butler McVay III's court-martial dishonored the crew, Bell said so himself, and he doesn't deserve to feel that way, because Maurice Bell is an honorable man who served his country and nearly died for it.

Even an eleven-year-old boy knows when something isn't fair. Hunter was looking for a topic for his project on the theme of Triumph and Tragedy, and now he knows he's found a good one.

He has no idea how far it's going to take him.

Chapter Three

Background: The Enemy
1914–1945

Shouting confusedly, they all began to scramble for the ships.
High in the air, a dust cloud from their scuffling rose, commands
rang back and forth — to man the cables, haul the black ships to
the salt immortal sea.

Homer, *The Iliad*

When World War II began, the world was in many ways unlike the world we know now. There was no television to watch, only radios to listen to. There were no satellites to provide us with instantaneous global communications. Information resided in books in libraries, not in computers where it could be summoned with a few clicks of a mouse. Air travel abroad was expensive and flights were limited. Compared to today, the countries of the earth were in many ways quite ignorant of one another. The enemy being faced and fought in the South Pacific by the likes of Maurice Bell or Captain Charles B. McVay III was to a great extent an unknown quantity.

19

During the First World War (1914–1918), Japan actually entered into an alliance with the United States and occupied German colonial holdings in China and in the South Pacific. In 1931, an explosion on the Japanese-owned South Manchuria Railroad, said to be caused by Chinese nationalists (some historians today think the explosion may have been set by the Japanese as an excuse), prompted the Japanese army to occupy all of Manchuria. On July 7, 1937, Japanese troops fought a Chinese patrol on the Marco Polo Bridge, twenty miles west of Beijing, a provocation the Japanese army used to justify occupying all of northern China, then advancing rapidly into eastern and southern China. When World War II broke out in Europe two years later, in the fall of 1939, Japan entered into a tripartite alliance with Germany and Italy, pledging mutual aid for the next ten years, then invaded French Indochina (modern-day Vietnam), claiming the invasion was purely for defensive purposes.

It seemed to outside observers that Japan's military aggression abroad was welcomed at home by the Japanese people. The October 29, 1929, crash of the U.S. Stock Exchange on "Black Friday" had plunged the entire world into a devastating economic depression, choking off Japanese trade with other countries, slowing Japanese industrial growth and increasing turmoil and unemployment in a country about the size of Montana. About half the population of 80,000,000 were peasants or fishermen living in relative poverty and deprivation. Under such conditions, a strong military provided both a sense of security and hope. Japanese politicians were talking about Japan leading the way toward a "Greater East Asia Co-Prosperity Sphere," fulfilling what seemed to them a kind of national destiny.

What Japan called a "Co-Prosperity Sphere," others called world domination. It became clear to the United States that Japan's expansionist policies included ambitions toward British, French and Dutch colonial holdings in Asia, including Hong Kong, Singapore and the Dutch East Indies. It also seemed logical that Japan was likely to move while England, France and the Netherlands were busy fighting Nazi Germany in Europe. U.S. representatives, directed by President Franklin Delano Roosevelt, made repeated efforts to negotiate with the Japanese to get them to pull their troops back, even though similar attempts to negotiate with Nazi Germany had met with disastrous results. To fortify his negotiating position, on July 26, 1941, President Roosevelt froze all of Japan's assets in the U.S., estimated at $131,000,000, and five days later, he banned the export of oil to Japan, which relied on the U.S. for 80 percent of the oil it consumed. Immediately, the Japanese naval chief of staff, Admiral Osami Nagano, went to Emperor Hirohito and recommended that Japan attack the United States. Admiral Isoroku Yamamoto, commander of the Combined Imperial Fleet, argued that the only answer to the American threat was a sudden massive attack against the U.S. naval forces currently being marshaled at Pearl Harbor, which he described as "a dagger pointed at our throats." The Japanese estimated that America's industrial might gave the U.S. ten times the production capacity of Japan. They hoped to deliver such a massive blow to U.S. armed forces at Pearl Harbor that, in the time it took America to recover and rebuild, Japan could establish a perimeter of fortified island bases in the Pacific, calculating that those bases would be strong enough to deter retaliation and force the U.S. to negotiate a settlement.

War became inevitable on October 23, 1941, when Japanese Prime Minister Prince Fumimaro Konoe, a pacifist, resigned. He was replaced as prime minister by the minister for war, fifty-seven-year-old extremist Hideki Tojo, a man whose nickname as an army officer had been "The Razor." Even as Japan continued diplomatic efforts to get the U.S. to release its oil, plans were drawn up to attack the American fleet at Pearl Harbor.

The surprise attack at Pearl came at 7:55 A.M. on Sunday, December

7, 1941. Japanese aircraft sank or damaged 8 battleships, 3 cruisers, 3 destroyers, 2 auxiliary ships, 1 mine layer and 1 target ship. They destroyed 188 aircraft on the ground and damaged 159 more, and they killed 2,330 American servicemen while wounding 1,347.

American losses at Pearl Harbor gave Japan a tremendous early advantage. At the same time that its planes were attacking Pearl, other forces moved against Malaysia, Thailand, the Philippines, Guam, Wake Island and Hong Kong. After only six months of fighting, Japan ruled over 1,000,000 square miles and 150,000,000 people in the Philippines, Malaysia, Singapore, Hong Kong, Sumatra, Java, Borneo, Burma and Thailand. Yet even as the U.S. built new ships to replace vessels lost in the attack on Pearl Harbor, the Japanese were finding out that they had won too much too fast. They lacked the qualified personnel needed to staff the factories, plantations and refineries they'd captured. They had trouble feeding the people in the countries they'd occupied because they couldn't replace food previously imported from the colonial powers. They had problems keeping their supply lines open because of the great distances involved and because they'd done little to protect their shipping. Their merchant ships became relatively easy targets for U.S. submarines.

The tide of the war turned at the Battle of Midway. From Midway Island, a two-square-mile U.S. possession 1,300 miles northwest of Hawaii, the Japanese hoped to gain control over the vast regions of the mid-Pacific. The massive naval battle began on June 4, 1942. By the time it was over, the Japanese fleet had lost 4 carriers, 1 cruiser, 322 planes and 3,500 men, while the U.S. lost only 1 carrier, 150 planes and 307 men. The Japanese also lost their sense of invincibility, and with it the hope that America might be willing to negotiate a peace settlement rather than pursue the war to its end.

One of the ships fighting on the American side since the beginning of the war was the USS *Indianapolis,* a heavy cruiser that served as the flagship for Rear Admiral Raymond Spruance, commander of the U.S. Fifth Fleet, an armada of about 200 ships. One of the older ships in the U.S. Navy at the time of the attack on Pearl Harbor, the *Indianapolis* was originally launched on November 7, 1931. She was 610 feet 4 inches long, or the length of two football fields, 66 feet 1 inch wide at the beam, displacing 9,600 tons and drawing 24 feet 10 inches when fully manned and provisioned, with eight White-Forster boilers driving four Parsons geared turbines producing 107,000 horsepower to turn four screws. Her hull was not protected with heavy armor, the way the hulls of battleships and carriers were, which left her vulnerable to attack from mines or torpedoes. Her light weight, however, made her one of the fastest ships in the navy, with a flank speed of 32 knots. She carried nine 8-inch guns capable of throwing 150-pound shells five miles, and four 5-inch guns, used to bombard Japanese island fortifications from two miles away in advance of U.S. landings. For defense, she sported twenty-four 40-mm intermediate range guns and thirty-two 20-mm Oerlikon antiaircraft guns. She also carried three SC-2 Curtis Seahawk airplanes used to scout out enemy positions. The *Indy*'s planes were launched from catapults, and after completing their missions, the seaplanes would land in the water, where they would be hoisted back up to the deck by cranes, located in a gap amidships, and stored in hangars. The gap amidships gave the *Indy* a somewhat swaybacked silhouette.

In April 1940 she'd moved from the West Coast to Hawaii with the rest of the Pacific Fleet but was out at sea on maneuvers when Pearl Harbor was attacked. Admiral Spruance chose her as his flagship not because she was the biggest or most powerful ship in the fleet but for her speed and maneuverability, and for her comfortable quarters. As commander of the Fifth Fleet, Spruance needed to be able to move quickly and independently between his various task forces, often sailing without escort.

In February of 1942, the *Indianapolis* participated in raids on

Bougainville, in the Solomon Islands, where elements of the Japanese Fourth Fleet had invaded hoping to gain access to the oil refineries of the Dutch East Indies. In the summer of 1943, she fought off the western Aleutian Islands, where the Japanese had captured portions of what would later become the state of Alaska. In November and December of that year, the *Indianapolis* was part of a 100-ship task force involved in Operation Galvanic, the code name for the invasion of the Gilbert Islands. Again and again, sailors on the *Indianapolis* witnessed the tenacity of Japanese resistance.

From the deck of the *Indy,* in January, February and March of 1944, Admiral Spruance commanded the U.S. invasion of the Marshall Islands, a 620-mile-long chain of 2,000 islands and islets that the Japanese needed to hold to protect their southern seas. The *Indianapolis* was at Palau, Yap, Ulithi and Woleai as, island by island, Allied forces moved closer and closer to the Japanese homelands. Every island captured by U.S. and Allied forces became a base, or an airfield, or a fuel depot, or a place to repair damaged ships and refuel and launch airplanes and house reinforcements.

It was at the Battle of the Philippine Sea, June 19–20, 1944, that the Japanese realized the war was essentially lost. The *Indianapolis* led Admiral Spruance's Task Force 58, which included fifteen aircraft carriers, against a Japanese fleet that included nine aircraft carriers. The Japanese lost 400 airplanes in dogfights over the Mariana Islands before the fleets themselves engaged, causing some to dub the battle "The Great Marianas Turkey Shoot." Spruance sent high-level bombers, dive-bombers and torpedo planes against the Japanese armada, American naval and air power sinking the carriers *Shokaku, Taiho* and *Hiyo,* as well as two destroyers and a tanker. Spruance's fleet suffered damage to two carriers, two battleships, one heavy cruiser and two destroyers before the Japanese withdrew. Once again, the *Indy* survived without a scratch. She sailed to Tinian, the first U.S. ship to enter the harbor where U.S. forces landed on July 24, 1944. In September, her crew found themselves in the western Carolines.

By the fall of 1944, in an effort to defend their country to the last full measure, the Japanese armed forces began using suicide bombers, including *kamikazes*. The word "kamikaze" translates as "divine wind," originally a reference to a typhoon that saved Japan from an invading Mongol fleet in 1281. The term referred, in 1944, to airplanes loaded with explosives that Japanese pilots crashed into Allied ships, destroying themselves in the process. The Japanese also deployed suicide speedboats packed with depth charges, and *kaitens,* which were manned torpedoes that could be steered into enemy ships. A kaiten that missed its target would simply sink to the bottom once its fuel was spent, killing the pilot either way.

As Allied forces closed in on Japan, two significant islands remained to be captured. The first was Iwo Jima, in the Volcano Islands, about 100 miles southeast of Kyushu, the southernmost of Japan's main islands. The second was Okinawa, only sixty miles away from Kyushu in the Ryukyu chain. For the first time, men aboard the *Indianapolis* began to allow themselves to think the war could be over in the not too distant future. The danger zone was, it seemed, growing smaller and smaller. Sailors on the *Indianapolis* even felt that their ship was a lucky ship. Sailors are notorious for their superstitions, and the men of the *Indianapolis* were no exception.

The fighting on Iwo Jima began on February 19, 1945, when 30,000 marines landed to face 21,500 Japanese troops dug into a network of underground fortifications. It was some of the most horrific fighting of the war. The *Indianapolis* sat offshore, assisting in the bombardment of enemy positions and, for the first time in the war, using its antiaircraft guns to fend off kamikaze attacks. Small pockets of Japanese resistance held out in Iwo Jima until March 26, but the *Indy*'s job was finished. Once again, the *Indianapolis* emerged undamaged and intact, triumphant in her ninth major campaign.

Her luck would turn at Okinawa, the last stepping-stone before the invasion of the home islands. On the morning of March 18, Japanese planes attacked the *Indianapolis* and other ships in the fleet, and six planes were shot down, the *Indianapolis* destroying one by hitting it with 40-mm shells. Another cruiser in the fleet shot down a plane that splashed into the water just off the *Indianapolis*'s port side. The next afternoon two Japanese planes were shot down, one by the *Indianapolis*, its men cheering as the plane burst into flames. On March 25, the *Indianapolis* began bombarding Okinawa from twelve miles offshore. As the ship gradually drew closer in, sailors with binoculars could see what remained of homes and terraced gardens. They could also see Okinawan civilians jumping from cliffs, committing suicide in advance of the American invasion.

The dawn of Saturday, March 31, broke gray. Around seven o'clock, a lookout on the bridge of the *Indianapolis* saw a plane come out of the clouds, heading straight for the *Indy*. An alert sounded. A gunner at the bow began firing. Tracers intercepted the plane's path, some scoring direct hits. The plane kept coming. Cozell Smith ran for the gunnery station called the "bathtub," swung the big gun around and fired off a steady stream of bullets. The plane bore down and hit the ship. One wing struck the bathtub, knocking Smith off his feet. The plane's motor pierced the main deck and exited through the side of the ship. Pieces of the plane scattered over the deck, which was quickly slick with oil and aviation fuel. Pieces of the pilot scattered across the deck as well. Two of the three observation planes were wrecked. Four men were thrown over the side.

The plane also carried an armor-piercing bomb with a delayed detonator. The bomb penetrated the reinforced-steel main deck and passed through the number three mess hall, shattering a table where a group had just finished eating. One man was killed in the mess hall, and a dozen were injured. The bomb pierced two more decks and lodged in a compartment where it struck the port propeller shaft. It exploded, blowing a hole in the side of the ship. Several compartments flooded as seawater rushed in. Immediately damage control officers gave orders to fasten the hatch doors leading to the damaged compartments. Some men managed to scramble out, wet and covered with fuel oil. Others didn't get to the hatchways in time. On a ship in danger of sinking, when the order is given to close the hatches, the hatches are closed regardless of who gets caught behind them. Eight men were trapped in the flooded compartments. Including the sailor who died in the mess hall, nine men were dead and fifteen were wounded.

Kamikaze attacks continued even as the *Indianapolis* sailed to the nearby island of Kerama-Retto for further repairs, more terrifying than anything the crew of the *Indianapolis* had yet encountered, suicidal madmen falling out of the sky. The Japanese defense of Okinawa grew more desperate. Japanese soldiers were swimming out to Allied ships to throw grenades at them. On the night of April 3, a Japanese soldier climbed aboard the *Indianapolis,* slashed a marine with a knife and then disappeared.

The next day the news came that Admiral Spruance, his staff and some of the crew would be transferring to the USS *New Mexico*. The rest of the crew would sail the *Indianapolis* back to San Francisco for repairs at the Mare Island shipyard. On the passage to Mare, feelings aboard ship were mixed. The grief they all felt for the nine shipmates lost in the kamikaze attack gave way to relief. They were heading home, back to San Francisco for a little rest and recreation, a chance to eat real food and go to the movies or see loved ones. Yet some men talked of putting in for transfers to other ships because the *Indy* was jinxed, they said—her luck had run out. Their friends scolded them for being superstitious, but it was a hard feeling to shake.

Chapter Four

The Men
June 1945

We few, we happy few, we band of brothers;
For he today that sheds his blood with me
Shall be my brother. . . .

William Shakespeare, *Henry V*

While the ship was being repaired, some men went home on leave to see their families, their friends or their sweethearts. Others had to stay to help with the repair work. Damages inflicted by the kamikaze pilot at Okinawa were extensive. The *Indy* also needed a fresh coat of paint, a new camouflage design.

In the daily papers, in the newsreels shown before the feature films in movie theaters, and in dinner party conversations at the base, hope rose that the war would be over soon, coupled with a measured despair at what it was going to cost to end it. The planned invasion of Japan was called Operation Downfall, and it came in two parts. First would be Operation Olympic, aimed at the southernmost main island of Kyushu, scheduled for November 1, 1945. Operation Coronet, aimed at the northernmost main island of Honshu, was scheduled for March 1, 1946. Smaller islands nearby would have to be taken first, and air bases built on them. Operation Coronet would send 22 Allied combat divisions against an expected 1,000,000 Japanese troops. American intelligence estimates anticipated 1,000,000 U.S. casualties by the fall of 1946; some intelligence staffers considered that a conservative estimate. The war would end, the officers of the *Indianapolis* knew, but at what horrible cost? If the invasion itself weren't dangerous enough, the scheduling of Operation Olympic for November meant the invasion would take place during typhoon season.

On July 4, even though repairs were still in progress, the *Indianapolis* held an open house, a chance for officers and crewmen to bring their families aboard for tours, to see where they lived and worked. The cooks served cake and ice cream. Crewmen gave away souvenirs, *Indianapolis* buttons that the kids could pin to their shirts, even official United States Navy bars of soap. For some of the wives, it was their first opportunity to meet Captain McVay, the forty-six-year-old son of Admiral Charles Butler McVay, Jr., the former commander in chief of the U.S. Asiatic Fleet. They knew his service record, that the captain of the *Indianapolis* had been appointed to the Naval Academy by President Wilson and graduated in 1919. He'd won a Silver Star for conspicuous gallantry in 1943 as the executive officer on the cruiser USS *Cleveland*. He'd served as the chairman of the Joint Intelligence Committee of Combined Chiefs of Staff in Washington, D.C., where he briefed Allied admirals and generals. They'd heard the stories, that he'd married a Hawaiian princess, that after the divorce he'd dated Hollywood starlets until he married his current wife, Louise. He was liked by his men and respected by his officers. He was fair-minded, having ordered that there would be no movies shown aboard ship for his officers unless the enlisted men had them too. It was a small thing, perhaps, but the men appreciated it.

The next day, the news arrived that the *Indy* had been ordered to sail on July 16. Leaves were canceled. The exact nature of the mission was passed down the chain of command on a "need-to-know" basis, which meant that the enlisted men were left in the dark, which wasn't unusual. What was unusual was that this time, not even the senior officers knew what the mission was. Captain McVay was summoned to San Francisco and told to report to the office of Rear Admiral William R. Purnell. Along with Major General Leslie Groves of the Manhattan Project, America's top-secret nuclear weapons program, Purnell had decided the *Indianapolis* would be used to transport components of the first atomic bomb to the island of Tinian, where a silver B-29 dubbed the *Enola Gay* waited. A surface ship was chosen to transport the bomb because no one was quite certain yet what it would take to accidentally detonate it. There was a fear that if an airplane transporting the bomb crashed on takeoff, the city of San Francisco could be destroyed. Though it was only a transport mission, it was still one of the most important missions of the war. That the navy trusted Captain McVay with it indicated that they held him in high regard.

Joining Admiral Purnell at the briefing was Navy Captain William Sterling Parsons, whose job it would be to assemble the bomb on the *Enola Gay* en route to Hiroshima. McVay didn't need to know what Parsons would be assembling. He was told only that he'd be carrying "special cargo." He was to guard it with utmost care, and if for any reason his ship sank along the way, and somehow there was only one lifeboat available, the cargo was to be given the lifeboat. He was told he was to sail at flank speed, because every day he saved would cut the length of the war by that much.

Captain McVay told his officers what he knew. Most of the

common seamen knew only that they were heading back into the war, possibly gearing up for the invasion of the Japanese home islands.

Seaman First Class Robert McGuiggan was a twenty-two-year-old Irish kid from the north side of Chicago. He'd worked a variety of construction jobs before the war. He'd gone home to Chicago on leave and got engaged to a girl named Gloria. Aboard the *Indy,* he served as a gunner's mate on gun number eight and helped catapult scout planes off the ship. In his spare time he was fond of playing poker in the spud locker off the mess hall, where they kept and peeled the potatoes. The games were illegal, and you could draw fines or brig time for gambling, but even ensigns and warrant officers occasionally joined the games, dealing five-card draw and seven-card stud. McGuiggan was a good player, and he tried not to make a habit of beating the officers too badly.

Radio Technician Second Class Jack Miner was one of the new guys. He'd been a freshman at Yale but enlisted at eighteen to avoid being drafted. He'd gone to radio technician school and had joined the *Indianapolis* at Mare Island. There he hung out with other radio techs, though he was only nineteen and underage, unable to join them when they went to the bars of nearby Vallejo on shore leave. He spent his time at Mare familiarizing himself with the ship, taking inventory of its radio equipment, learning how to operate it and where all the wires went, busy every minute of the day. He was excited to ship out on a cruiser, a fast, swashbuckling, athletic sort of vessel, he thought.

Mike Kuryla was a coxswain from Chicago, a veteran sailor who'd seen a lot of men die, a participant in eight major battles and plenty of smaller battles in between. He'd enlisted young and he'd been trained well, which meant he was taught to kill. His duties included basic ship maintenance and manning the 5-inch guns. In his spare time he spliced line, made knots, jumped rope for exercise or tossed around a medicine ball. He liked to listen to baseball on the radio when they could get it, or to the Texas and Louisiana boys aboard ship playing guitar and mandolin, or sometimes the Polish boys from Detroit and Chicago playing polkas on their accordions. He stayed away from the card games but could occasionally be found below decks shooting craps on a blanket, throwing dice against the bulkhead in some corner of the ship with the other coxswains and bosun's mates while somebody stood lookout in the hall.

Ship's Cook First Class Morgan Moseley was also a seasoned tar. Morgan had quit school after the sixth grade to support his mother and sister. He'd worked as a sharecropper, plowing forty acres behind a mule when he was twelve years old, later hiring on with the railroad. He was on his way to church when he heard about Pearl Harbor. He joined the navy, went to boot camp in San Diego and then spent four months in cook school, joining the crew of the *Indianapolis* in May of 1943. He'd been working in the galley when the kamikaze plane hit the *Indy* at Okinawa, crashing through the galley and then the mess hall, killing nine men and chipping one of Moseley's teeth.

Ensign Harlan Twible was a new officer, the son of a mill-worker from Gilbertville, Massachusetts. His father was an Irish immigrant who taught his children not to take for granted the opportunities or the freedoms their adopted country offered. Harlan was working his way through the University of Massachusetts when he passed a test

that made him eligible for the Naval Academy. He took his appoint-
ment seriously, entered in 1941, studied hard and finished in three
years. At Mare, Twible familiarized himself with his new ship and duties. He was the last officer to come on board, and a bit disappointed,
having hoped to become either a pilot or a submariner, but he respected the authority of those above him and agreed to go where he
was needed. "You're Naval Academy and we expect a lot from you,"
Captain McVay had said when he reported in. His duty station was sky
aft, the secondary gunnery control atop a 100-foot-tall observation
tower connected by telephone to the bridge, where he'd be in charge of
the aft guns. It seemed like a lot of responsibility to give to a green ensign fresh out of the academy, but he was determined to learn his job
and do his duty. He tried to have faith in the *Indianapolis,* but nevertheless sensed a certain aura about it that he couldn't put his finger
on, something that made him oddly apprehensive.

Giles McCoy was a ruggedly handsome twenty-one-year-old
marine from St. Louis, the son of a butter salesman who'd fought in
World War I. He was a pugnacious young man with a strong sense of
justice, and used to beat up the bullies at school who picked on
younger kids. He'd been a star athlete in high school, a shortstop with
hopes of playing in the major leagues. He joined the marines in June
of 1943 because they were supposed to be the toughest guys in the
service. Marines were trained to provide security aboard ships and to
go ashore in landing parties and fight, more like soldiers than sailors.

On the *Indianapolis,* McCoy, in addition to pulling guard duty,
served as Captain McVay's personal orderly, bodyguard and message
runner. When Admiral Spruance was on board, it was McCoy's job to
accompany the admiral on his daily constitutionals and make sure he
didn't fall overboard. He found Captain McVay to be serious, polite, a

real gentleman, somewhat formal but generally nice, a man McCoy liked and respected. McVay seemed to like him in return, because McCoy kept his shoes shined and his slacks pressed and stood at attention and did his job—when the captain gave him a message, he never had to repeat it.

McCoy went into San Francisco on liberty one night with three of his buddies while the ship was being repaired. They didn't have enough money to get into any real trouble, but they did their best under the circumstances. They were walking down the sidewalk in their dress whites when one of them flicked his cigarette to the ground and it landed upright, standing on end, smoking like a chimney. The four stared in disbelief.

"Well, you know what that means," a second man said.

"What?" the first one asked.

"It's an omen," the second man joked. "It means you're going to get it when we go back out."

The others laughed.

Chapter Five

The Mission
July 1945

The young men falling in and arming,
The mechanics arming, (the trowel, the jack-plane, the blacksmith's
hammer, tossed aside with precipitation,)
The lawyer leaving his office and arming, the judge leaving the court,
The driver deserting his wagon in the street, jumping down, throwing the
reins abruptly down on the horses' backs,
The salesman leaving the store, the boss, the book-keeper, porter, all leaving;
Squads gather everywhere by common consent and arm,
The new recruits, even boys, the old men show them how to wear their
accoutrements, they buckle the straps carefully. . . .

Walt Whitman, "First O Songs for a Prelude"

On Sunday, July 15, the *Indianapolis* sailed from Mare Island, traveling south twenty-five miles to Hunters Point naval shipyard, just across the water from where Candlestick Park stands today. That afternoon, two nondescript army trucks pulled up alongside the ship. Sailors looking over the side to the pier below saw officers and armed guards and knew that something important was coming aboard, whatever it was. One team unloaded a large wooden crate, about fifteen feet long. "Probably whiskey for the admirals," one sailor joked. Another thought it was full of money. A second team off-loaded a heavy 200-pound cylinder, about two feet high and eighteen inches in diameter, resembling a fat lead wastebasket. Traveling with the bomb, though only they knew it was a bomb, were an intelligence expert in atomic energy and an M.D. serving as medical overseer. His job was to monitor the cylinder with a Geiger counter for radiation leaks from the uranium 235 inside, an amount equal, in explosive power, to about 30,000,000 pounds of dynamite.

The *Indianapolis* received one other shipment of note at Hunters Point, a new supply of kapok life jackets, 2,500 of them, which was all well and good, except that the ship only carried a crew of about 1,200 men. Such mix-ups were not uncommon in the military, but it only added to the chaos aboard ship. Places had to be found to store the extra life preservers, usually stashed in hanging bags along the bulkhead. There also were 50 Mare Island shipyard workers sailing as far as Pearl Harbor to finish their repairs en route, in addition to 100 other passengers traveling to various destinations in the Pacific, all of whom needed to be housed and fed. McVay had 250 new crew members to train, inexperienced sailors who had to be put through fire drills and abandon ship drills and in general shown their duties and responsibilities. Usually he tried to greet his new recruits by name, but this would take some time. Thirty of his eighty officers were new as well. Training would be no easy task with so many passengers loafing about to get in the way. McVay had much to do to get the *Indy* in fighting trim before Admiral Spruance returned to his flagship.

She sailed from Hunters Point on July 16. In 1932, the USS *Omaha* had set a record by sailing between San Francisco and Honolulu in 75.4 hours, a record the *Indianapolis* broke by over an hour, arriving at Pearl the morning of the fourth day. After a quick six-hour layover to debark passengers, refuel and let her engines cool, the *Indianapolis* put out to sea again and headed for Tinian, 3,300 miles to the west.

Tinian was a forty-square-mile coral island, once home to a large and heavily fortified Japanese base that was taken by U.S. forces exactly a year before. Now that it was in U.S. possession, it was home to one of the busiest airfields in the world, the staging area for air raids on Japan. The *Indy* averaged twenty-four knots for this leg of the trip and finally dropped anchor offshore on July 26. There she received the following order:

> DATE: 26 July 1945
> FROM: CINCPAC Adv Hq
> TO: Indianapolis
>
> Upon completion unloading Tinian report to Port Director for routing to Guam where disembark Com. 5th Fleet personnel X Completion report to PD Guam for onward routing to Leyte where on arrival report CTF 95 by dispatch for duty X CTG 95.7 directed arrange 10 days training for Indianapolis in Leyte Area.

CINCPAC (pronounced "sink-pack") stood for "Commander in Chief, Pacific," the post held by four-star Fleet Admiral Chester W. Nimitz. His main headquarters were in Hawaii, but his advance headquarters were in Guam, a short sail from Tinian. The directive ordered McVay to visit the port director at Tinian for routing instructions, and then to sail to Guam. The order didn't specify the date, and said only that McVay was to sail to Guam "upon completion unloading," meaning whenever he was finished unloading whatever it was he had to unload (the order didn't mention the atomic bomb, needless to say, because that was top-secret). "Disembark Com. 5th Fleet personnel" meant McVay was to drop off his passengers in Guam. After that, he was to report to the PD or port director at the Guam naval base for routing west across the Philippine Sea to the island of Leyte, Philippines. Upon reaching Leyte, McVay was to send a message saying he'd arrived to CTF 95 or Commander, Task Force 95, a fleet of ships then operating in the waters off Japan, led by Vice Admiral Jesse B. Oldendorf aboard the USS *Omaha*. The last sentence of the order tells McVay that CTG 95.7 or Commander, Task Group 95.7 had been directed to arrange for ten days of gunnery training in the Leyte area. Task Group 95.7 was led by Rear Admiral Lynde D. McCormick, whose flag flew on the battleship USS *Idaho*.

Copies of the order were also sent to the port director at Tinian, to Commander Brooks, the port director at Guam, to Vice Admiral George Murray, who was the head of the Marianas command with the responsibility of overseeing the area the *Indianapolis* had sailed from, and to Admirals Nimitz, Spruance and Oldendorf—seven copies, telling seven different people or offices what the *Indianapolis* was going to be doing and where it would be traveling. The *Indianapolis* arrived in Guam on July 27, then home to nearly 500,000 troops waiting to hit the beaches of Japan proper. At CINCPAC's advance headquarters in Guam, Captain McVay met with Commodore James B. Carter, Admiral Nimitz's assistant chief of staff. Carter told McVay he could sail the next morning. McVay left Commodore Carter's office at CINCPAC believing, from the man's words and tone, that nothing much was going on in this part of the war, a sensibility Admiral Spruance confirmed when he told McVay over lunch that "Nothing big was in the wind." Spruance said he was not yet certain whether or not he'd ride with the *Indianapolis* to the Philippines or fly.

At 4 P.M., Captain McVay reported to the port director's office,

only to find Commander Brooks out. McVay met instead with Lieutenant Joseph Waldron, the convoy and routing officer. About 90 percent
of the ships leaving the Marianas had been routed by Waldron, around
5,000 ships in the last ten months. McVay assumed Waldron knew what
he was doing. He asked Waldron what speed he wanted him to travel at.
A fleet order at the time recommended that ships without time con-
straints travel at a speed of sixteen knots to save fuel. McVay had two
concerns. He wanted, first, to rest his engines a bit after two high-speed
runs, one from San Francisco to Pearl and another from Pearl to Tinian,
and second, he wanted to arrive in Leyte at dawn. A speed of twenty-five
knots would have put him in Leyte on Monday morning, but that was
too fast. Arriving in Leyte on Tuesday meant leaving at 9 A.M. Saturday
morning, July 28, and traveling at 15.7 knots.

The next thing to be decided was the route. This was somewhat
simpler. Wartime Pacific routing instructions stated, "Under normal pro-
cedures, combatant fleet components proceeding to or returning from
combat areas shall be sailed on standard routes whenever such routes are
available." The standard route to Leyte, sailing west from Guam, was a
direct line called "Convoy Route Peddie." Peddie it was then.

McVay next asked for an escort ship. The *Indianapolis* was not
equipped with sonar, and therefore had no way to detect enemy submarines. Ordinarily, ships without antisubmarine capabilities were accompanied by destroyer escorts, which carried sonar equipment and
depth charges and which had proven quite adept at deterring submarine
attacks. Waldron called the office of Vice Admiral Murray at Commander Marianas, and was put through to the surface operations officer, one
Captain Oliver Naquin. Naquin, however, was out of his office.
Waldron spoke instead to Naquin's assistant, a Lieutenant Johnson,
who told Waldron no escort was needed. The war had moved far north
of Guam, and most of the hostile actions were now concentrated in the
waters off the Japanese main islands. The Peddie route crossed what was

widely considered the "backwaters" of the war. For his part, McVay had sailed unescorted many times before, often with Admiral Spruance on board, and often in waters apparently more dangerous than the ones he was about to cross. He recognized that as the war drew to a close, escorts were needed more in forward areas, both to escort ships and to rescue pilots who splashed into the sea flying missions over Japan. If no escort was available, he would make do, even though the *Indianapolis* would be the first capital ship (cruisers, battleships and aircraft carriers were all categorized as capital ships) to sail from Guam to Leyte unescorted since the war had begun.

That evening, three hours later, around seven o'clock, the *Indianapolis*'s navigation officer, Commander Janney, met with Waldron and was handed two reports, first the routing instructions and then an intelligence briefing. Janney studied them. The routing instructions contained the essential travel details, that the ship was to leave at 9 A.M. July 28, sail 1,171 miles west-southwest to Leyte at a speed of 15.7 knots, arriving in Leyte at 11 A.M. Tuesday morning, July 31. Clause 6 of the routing instructions read:

> Commanding Officers are at all times responsible for the safe navigation of their ships. They may depart from prescribed routing when, in their judgment, weather, currents or other navigational hazards jeopardize the safety of the ship. They will return to the prescribed route as soon as safety permits. Zigzag at discretion of Commanding Officer.

The phrase "Zigzag at discretion of Commanding Officer" meant that Captain McVay was allowed to use his own judgment whether or not to steer a course that constantly changed, or zigzagged, as a way of evading possible attack by enemy submarine torpedoes. It was customary for U.S. ships' captains to zigzag during daylight hours and at night in times of good visibility, though many captains chose to cease zigzagging at night under conditions of poor visibility. The reason to zigzag was, of course, that if an enemy torpedo was coming straight at a ship, changing course would take it out of harm's way. On the other hand, submarines usually fired more than one torpedo at a time in a spread pattern, such that zigzagging was in some cases as likely to steer a ship into the path of one torpedo as out of the path of another. Many ships' captains were aware that during the war, U.S. submarine commanders had sunk over 4,000 enemy ships, most of which were zigzagging. The value of zigzagging had been debated since the war began. At any rate, the routing instructions, which superseded any other sailing orders, left it up to Captain McVay. His decision whether or not to stop zigzagging at night would be informed in part by the weather and the visibility on any given night, and in part by the degree of threat from enemy submarine activities. For that, he would rely on the intelligence report Waldron gave Janney.

The danger seemed low. The intelligence report listed only three submarine sightings, none of them particularly ominous. There'd been a surface submarine on July 22, but that news was six days old, and the sighting had taken place 700 miles from the Peddie route. The intelligence brief also mentioned two rather dubious July 25 reports, first an "Unknown ship" reporting they'd sighted a "possible periscope at 13:56N–135:56E," the second telling Commander Janney of a "Sound contact reported at 10:30N–136:25E," but that "Indications at that time pointed to a doubtful submarine." This was about 100 miles south of the Peddie route, arguably along the *Indianapolis*'s course, but all told, phrases like "unknown ship" and "possible periscope" and "doubtful submarine" didn't set off any alarms. There'd been lots of false reports during the war, nervous merchant ships' captains seeing threats in the darkness.

The night before sailing was uncomfortably warm. For all her speed and grace, the *Indy* was not a particularly well-ventilated ship, a situation that posed a problem when the ship was sailing in humid tropical climes. She often sailed with her hatches open below to allow the passage of air, but even so men frequently chose to sleep topside wherever they could.

On Saturday morning, Spruance informed Captain McVay he wouldn't be boarding the *Indianapolis* for the trip to the Philippines. Promptly at 9 A.M., the *Indianapolis* hoisted anchor and departed for Leyte. At 10:40 that morning, Lieutenant Waldron's office transmitted a message containing the essential travel details, that the ship left Guam at 9 A.M., July 28, averaging 15.7 knots on the Peddie route, and that it was due to arrive in Leyte at approximately 8 A.M. Tuesday, July 31, dropping anchor at 11 A.M.

Waldron's message also indicated that the *Indianapolis* would be sailing between two control zones, leaving the Marianas command area and crossing over from east to west into the Philippine Sea Frontier at 130 degrees east longitude, the line between the two command zones usually referred to as "the Chop." The crossover would happen sometime Monday, Waldron's message said. Again, several copies of the message were sent: one to the shipping control officer, Marianas area; one to Lieutenant Commander Jules Sancho, who was the port director in Leyte; one to Rear Admiral McCormick of Task Group 95.7; and copies classified for "information" only forwarded to Admiral Spruance, Commodore Carter, Fleet Admiral Nimitz, Vice Admiral Murray and Vice Admiral Oldendorf. Both the Marianas command and the Philippine Sea Frontier had plotting boards to keep track of ship movements, and each was supposed to take the information Waldron had sent them and use it to follow the *Indianapolis* as she made her way from Guam to Leyte. Keeping track of a ship on a known straight-line route at a given

Harlan M. Twible, ensign,
USS *Indianapolis.*
(Courtesy of Harlan Twible)

Herbert J. Miner II,
radio technician
second class,
USS *Indianapolis.*
(Courtesy of Herbert Miner)

Morgan M. Moseley, seaman
first class, USS *Indianapolis.*
(Courtesy of Morgan Moseley)

Cozell Smith, coxswain,
USS *Indianapolis.*
(Courtesy of Diane Smith)

Maurice Glen Bell, seaman first class, USS *Indianapolis*. (Courtesy of Maurice Bell)

Michael N. Kuryla, coxswain, USS *Indianapolis*. (Courtesy of Michael Kuryla)

Robert McGuiggan, seaman
first class, USS *Indianapolis*.
(Courtesy of Robert and Gloria
McGuiggan)

Giles McCoy, private first class,
United States Marine Corps.
(Courtesy of Giles McCoy)

Members of the *Indianapolis* crew out on the town on their last leave before the final voyage. The arrows point to Robert McGuiggan (left) and Michael N. Kuryla (right), the only two sailors in this picture to survive the sinking.
(Courtesy of Robert and Gloria McGuiggan)

Michael N. Kuryla (left), Robert McGuiggan (center), and an unidentified survivor after the sinking.
(Courtesy of Robert and Gloria McGuiggan)

Charles Butler McVay III, captain, USS *Indianapolis*. (Courtesy of Betsy McVay)

Captain McVay tells war correspondents on Guam of the sinking of the USS *Indianapolis*. (National Archives)

Mochitsura Hashimoto, lieutenant commander, *I-58* submarine.
(Courtesy of Mochihiro Hashimoto)

Survivors of the sinking being taken to the hospital after their rescue. (National Archives)

rate of speed should have been a fairly simple undertaking, a question of moving a marker a few inches on a map every couple of hours.

At 4 P.M. Saturday, the day the *Indianapolis* hoisted anchor, a report came into the Marianas command from a merchant ship called the SS *Wild Hunter,* sailing for Manila carrying army cargo. The captain of the *Wild Hunter* was a man named Anton Wie, a seasoned professional. His position was seventy-five miles south of the Peddie route, and he said he'd seen a periscope. Twenty-eight minutes later a second emergency message from SS *Wild Hunter* reported that it had spotted the periscope again and this time fired two shots at it from a range of about 2,000 to 2,200 yards. An antisubmarine "hunter-killer group" was sent to investigate, comprised of spotter airplanes and the destroyer escort USS *Albert T. Harris.*

The next night at dinner, Commander Janney mentioned that he'd overheard ship-to-ship radio traffic about the *Wild Hunter* and the *Albert T. Harris* and the hunter-killer group activity. Jack Janney told those at his table quite casually that they'd probably pass the area where the *Wild Hunter* had spotted the periscope sometime around midnight. Again, no one was overly concerned. Erroneous reports of submarine sightings were commonplace.

McVay exercised his discretion at about 7:30 that night and gave the officer of the deck, Lieutenant Charles McKissick, the order to secure from zigzagging. From the navigation bridge, gazing forward past the fire control deck and the two 8-inch gun turrets with their 25-foot-long barrels, McVay saw that the seas were choppy and the sky was overcast. It was, in McVay's opinion, a night of good solid darkness, in waters that were, according to the best information he had, relatively safe. The ship also sped up to 17 knots to maintain the desired 15.7 average. The faster a ship sailing in a straight line traveled, the safer it was. Lieutenant McKissick was relieved as officer of the deck at 8:00 by Lieutenant

(Junior Grade) Keith MacFarland, who found the seas choppy with long swells rolling in from the southeast under "very dark" skies. Sharing the bridge on the eight to midnight shift with MacFarland were the supervisor of the watch, Commander Stanley Lipski, chief engineering officer Lieutenant Richard B. Redmayne and Quartermaster Third Class Vincent Allard, who noted in the log that it was so dark that he couldn't recognize people on the bridge.

Between 8:00 and 8:30, Commander Janney visited the bridge to drop off the night orders, which described the desired course and speed and stated that if there were any changes in weather or sea conditions, or any radar contacts, they were to wake and notify Captain McVay. Janney reported again that there was a hunter-killer group up ahead searching for an enemy submarine.

"We should pass the area around midnight," he said. They'd heard such reports before and nothing had ever come of them. As the ship cut through the darkness, Quartermaster Third Class Allard made notes in the deck log: "Moonrise 10:30 . . . altostratus clouds at medium altitude . . . cirrostratus at high . . . nothing at low altitude . . . total amount of sky covered, in tenths—six."

Captain McVay came on the bridge at 10:45. He reviewed and signed the night orders. He'd gone over Lieutenant Waldron's intelligence reports with Commander Janney. Having directed his men to wake him if conditions changed, trusting that his officers were competent and capable, he went to bed in his emergency cabin, not far from the bridge, where he could sleep with a voice tube at his ear if anyone needed to call him. He'd given his own cabin to a friend from the Naval Academy whom he'd met on Guam, a Captain Edwin Crouch who was on his way to the Philippines.

It was hot and humid below as the ship, a mere twelve degrees from the equator in midsummer, traveled in what was called "Condition Yoke Modified," which meant that the air ducts and most of the watertight doors on the second deck were left open to cool things off below. Many of the other doors and hatches below decks were open as well. Men carried mattresses topside, or blankets, anything to sleep on, if they could find a space. An eleven- to sixteen-knot breeze was blowing up from the southwest.

At midnight, Lieutenant John "Jack" Orr relieved Lieutenant MacFarland as the officer of the deck, and damage control officer Lieutenant Commander K. C. Moore relieved Lipski as supervisor of the watch. For a moment, the four men stood together, assessing the situation. Visibility was about 3,000 yards, somewhat improved from before, but the question was, had it improved enough to warrant waking the captain? At midnight, there were thirteen men on bridge, including a coxswain, a quartermaster, a helmsman, messengers, even a bugler, whose job it was to sound the alarm if the ship's communications were to fail. Men on watch strained their eyes against the darkness, a moon slightly better than a quarter full, sporadically shining down through the cloud cover directly behind them to the east. To the west, there was only darkness. To some it may have seemed like they were the only ship on the sea.

They weren't.

A Japanese sub lay directly ahead.

Chapter Six

The Sinking
July 30, 1945

I have wrestled with death. It is the most unexciting contest you can imagine. It takes place in an impalpable greyness, with nothing underfoot, with nothing around, without spectators, without clamour, without glory, without the great desire of victory, without the great fear of defeat, in a sickly atmosphere of tepid skepticism, without much belief in your own right, and still less in that of your adversary.

Joseph Conrad, *Heart of Darkness*

The enemy sub's identification number was *I-58*, and she'd been in service a mere ten months. She carried a crew of seventy-eight. To sink the *Indianapolis*, she had two weapons to choose from. She was armed with nineteen new oxygen-fueled wakeless T-95 torpedoes, each with a range of 3.5 miles at 48 knots, or 5.5 miles at 42 knots, delivering a payload of 1,210 pounds of explosive charge, fired from six forward torpedo tubes. She also carried six kaitens, the underwater equivalent of Japan's kamikaze planes.

The *I-58* was state-of-the-art Japanese technology. She displaced 3,000 tons when submerged. She was 355 feet long, 30 feet abeam, and could cruise at 14 knots submerged and 17 on the surface. She could safely dive to 120 meters (390 feet). The *I-58* had a soft rubber coating on the outer hull, so that sonar pings didn't bounce off it in the pattern of a ship, creating instead the sonar image of a whale or a school of fish that would, it was hoped, fool American sonar operators. She also had a type 1M3 radar, used to search the skies for aircraft, a type 2M2 radar used to search for surface ships, and two types of sonar, one acoustic and the other electric.

The captain of the *I-58* was Mochitsura Hashimoto, a thirty-six-year-old son of a Shinto priest, born in Kyoto. He was a 1931 graduate of the Japanese Naval Academy and had served as torpedo officer on the sub *I-24* when it was part of a five-submarine squadron lurking in the waters off Hawaii during the attack on Pearl Harbor. By July of 1945, Hashimoto had any number of reasons to feel dismay. His country was under daily bombardment, the war effort looking hopeless. The once proud Japanese Navy had only four big attack submarines left, three transport subs and eight obsolete subs that carried only two kaitens each. His personal record as captain of the *I-58* was less than stellar, claiming one unconfirmed tanker hit off Guam and not a single kill in action off Okinawa, where his ship had been under constant harassment the previous spring. Since he'd left base at Kure on July 16 under orders to harass enemy communications and attack enemy ships off the Philippines, diving during daylight hours and surfacing at night to hunt, Hashimoto had only managed to fire two kaitens at a tanker, both of which missed, their pilots perishing for nothing. On Wednesday, July 18, under a bright moon, he'd waited on the Saipan-Okinawa route but found no targets. Beginning Sunday, July 22, he'd waited on the Leyte-Guam route, the Peddie route the Americans called it, praying at the Shinto shrine in his quarters for an enemy ship to sink before the moon waned.

The weather on Sunday, July 29, had been bad all day, the skies cloudy, promising poor hunting. By nightfall, visibility was zero. He dove to await moonrise, turning in for a nap and waking at 10:30. At 11:00, he gave the order for night-action stations, cruising at a depth of 60 feet, speed 3 knots, night periscope up. He took a reading, sweeping his periscope a full 360 degrees. To the east, he saw a moon still low in the sky, a little more than a quarter full. In that direction, he could almost see a horizon.

"*Hujyoo seyo,*" he said. ("Surface.")

"*Barasuto o kara ni seyo.*" ("Blow main ballast.")

"*Sentoo-taisei ni tsuke.*" ("Action Stations.")

One sonar man thought he heard a ship, perhaps as far as 20,000 meters off, a distance of about 12 miles. Over the hydrophones, it sounded like somebody doing the dishes. When the *I-58* surfaced, navigator Lieutenant Hiromu Tanaka went topside, climbing to the bridge of the conning tower to scan the horizon with powerful binoculars. With great excitement Tanaka shouted, "*Tekikan o akai kyuujyuu-do hookoo ni hakken.*" ("Bearing red nine-zero degrees, possible enemy ship.")

When Hashimoto climbed to the bridge and picked up the binoculars, he saw a black dot on the horizon, about 10,000 meters off, a distance of slightly better than 6 miles. His pulse quickened. The moon was directly behind the ship, which seemed to be sailing straight toward him. Had the moon been anywhere else in the sky, he probably wouldn't have spotted the ship—it was almost a freak occurrence, that the moon would come out from behind the clouds just then, directly behind a ship, in the middle of the open ocean. It seemed like providence. For once, he was in the right place at the right time. He gave the order to dive.

"*Tekikan o kakunin. Gyorai o yooi. Kaiten o jyunbi seyo.*" ("Ship in sight. All tubes to the ready. Kaitens stand by.")

For a moment, the fact that the *Indianapolis* was heading straight toward him concerned him. What if he'd been detected, and the ship was a destroyer coming to attack him? A ship coming straight at him presented a very narrow profile and would be extremely difficult to hit. If only it would zigzag, he could get a better look at it.

When the *Indianapolis* was 4,000 meters away, about 2.5 miles, Hashimoto turned his ship to starboard and moved south. From his new perspective, he estimated the height of the *Indianapolis*'s masts at about 90 feet. That told him he was looking at a capital ship, either a battleship or a large cruiser. Knowing the size of the ship, he could compute her speed by counting the engine rotations through his hydrophones. He estimated her speed at 20 knots, or 23 miles per hour. As the *Indianapolis* drew closer, coming within 2,000 meters, he revised his estimates and figured she was doing about 12 knots, or almost 14 miles per hour.

At 11:54 P.M., he ordered six torpedoes readied, set at a depth of 4 meters, speed 48 knots.

"*Ichi ni tsuke,*" he said, staring through his periscope. ("Stand by.")

"*Ute!*" he said. ("Fire!")

Within fifteen seconds, six torpedoes were on their way, launched with a spread of 3 degrees in a fan pattern. Hashimoto waited. It would take a torpedo traveling 48 knots (approximately 60 miles per hour) about a minute to travel the 1,500 meters to the ship.

At 12:02, Captain Mochitsura Hashimoto looked through his periscope and saw a column of water shoot up into the sky near the front of his target, followed by tongues of red flame lighting up the darkness.

"*Meecyuu!*" he said. ("A hit!")

A few seconds later, he witnessed a second explosion.

"*Meecyuu!*" he repeated.

• • •

Mike Kuryla had gotten off watch a few minutes before midnight. With his buddy Paul, a fellow coxswain who'd taught him how to roller-skate one shore leave, he'd leaned against the splinter shield and sipped coffee, staring down at the water below. When the moon came out from behind the clouds, they could see the wake the ship made, and the black waves rolling endlessly on. Kuryla drained his coffee, took his shoes off, lay down on his back with his shoes under his head as a pillow, and was just closing his eyes when suddenly, his whole body stung, the way a batter's hands sting hitting a baseball with a cracked bat. His ears rang. A second explosion sent him flying. He sat up, saw smoke and flames between him and his forward battle station. He quickly manned the 5-inch gun where he was, training it out to sea, but there was no enemy in sight. Maybe the boilers had blown, he thought. Maybe they'd hit a mine. Maybe they'd been torpedoed.

Jack Miner had liberated a cot and crawled off to sleep in his underwear in what was referred to as "Battle II," the backup command center that would be used if the main bridge were ever knocked out of commission. The portholes were open and a breeze blew in, a delightful spot for sleeping, he thought.

Morgan Moseley had a terrible cold and hadn't eaten a thing all day. He was in charge of the galley, the bakeshop, the butcher shop and cold storage, and had spent the entire day Saturday cleaning because there was to be an inspection on Sunday. His quarters were three decks down, beneath the mess hall, just aft of midship. He was in bed when an explosion knocked him out of his bunk. He'd just gotten to his feet when the second explosion hit the ship.

Harlan Twible had spent the afternoon writing letters to his new bride and to his parents. He'd reported twenty minutes early (as was customary) for his second watch, 2000 to 2400 hours. There was nothing to be briefed about, no news, no sightings, gun mounts in good shape. Twible stared out to sea, but the skies were overcast and visibility was nil. It was so dark, in fact, that Twible had to leave his watch station to visit the aft guns below him to make sure they were manned. Ensign Donald Blum arrived to relieve him shortly before midnight. Twible briefed Blum on what had happened during his watch—nothing—mentioned that the ship was no longer zigzagging, commented on the darkness of the night and then descended from the sky aft tub. The first torpedo struck as he was descending, nearly knocking him off the ladder. He'd just hit the deck below when the second torpedo struck.

Gil McCoy was guarding the brig, where there were two prisoners. He'd reported thirty minutes early. The brig was as far aft as you could go, located in the very fantail of the ship, two levels below deck, and guarding it was one of the lousier duties a marine could pull, particularly on a hot, humid night, because there was no ventilation. Sometimes it seemed like there was no point, either—if somebody could break out of the brig, where were they going to go on a ship in the middle of the ocean? The brig opened onto a large room full of bunks where men slept and snored. McCoy was wishing he were topside when the torpedoes hit. The first torpedo exploded directly forward of the compartment in the bow where the thirty-nine-man marine detachment was quartered, killing everyone sleeping there. If McCoy hadn't reported early, he might have died with them. The first torpedo struck the *Indianapolis* on the starboard side (the right-hand side as you face forward) at about frame 7, ripping the first thirty to sixty-five feet of the ship off as easily as tearing the corner off an envelope. The explosion ignited a gas tank containing 3,500 gallons of highly volatile aviation fuel, the flames venting high in the air from the forward smokestack. The second torpedo, which slammed McCoy into the bulkhead and knocked the lights out in the brig, struck at about frame 50, amidships below the bridge, opening a large hole perhaps forty feet across and knocking out communications and all but emergency electrical power.

Captain McVay, who'd been asleep in his emergency cabin, first thought another kamikaze plane had found them. The second blast threw him from his bed. He then thought it could be mines—but they were too far out to sea for mines—or torpedoes, or perhaps his boilers had blown. His cabin filled with bitter white smoke. He hurried to the bridge, where he tried to make sense of the chaos all around him.

"Do you have any reports?" McVay asked.

"No, sir," Lieutenant Orr replied. "I've lost all communications. I tried to stop the engines but I don't know if the order got through to the engine rooms." (The engines in engine room 1 were destroyed, but engine room 2 was intact and operating.)

"Send word down to Radio one to get out a distress message. See what information you can get. Has anyone seen the damage control officer?" Instead of the damage control officer, Bugler First Class Donald Mack stepped forward.

"Reporting for duty."

"Stand by," Orr told him.

McVay ran to his cabin, quickly put on his pants, shoes and a shirt, then returned to the bridge. He was hoping he could still save the ship. He heard noises from below. Explosions. Bulkheads collapsing, one after the next, as the ship's engines drove her into the sea, mindlessly plowing forward, the bridge unable to communicate with anyone, as if the body of the ship had been separated from the head. With each collapsed bulkhead, the ship took on more water. There were higher-pitched sounds coming up from below as well, sounds of metal ripping, pipes shearing, electrical wires sparking, men screaming in pain. On deck, men hooked up fire hoses, only to find there was no water pressure. Damage control officer Lieutenant Commander Moore reported in.

"Forward compartments flooding fast. There are no repair parties there. We're badly damaged—do you want to abandon ship?"

McVay remembered the damage they'd sustained from the kamikaze pilot at Okinawa. They'd made it through that. Perhaps they could make it through this. He knew of other ships that had lost their bows and survived. It would be a big mistake to give the order to abandon ship until you were absolutely certain the ship was going to sink. Lives could be lost unnecessarily. Perhaps he was guilty of having too much faith in his ship, but she'd given him reason to have faith before on numerous occasions.

"No. I think we can hold her. Go below and check again and report back. Lieutenant Orr—any word from the radio room?"

"No sir, no word yet."

"Orders, sir?" Mack asked.

"Stand by."

"Bugler," McVay commanded, "check the inclinometer."

"Eighteen degrees to starboard, sir."

"Commander Janney," McVay said. "Get to the radios and send a message that we've been hit. Give position and say we're sinking rapidly, need immediate assistance."

"We've been damaged badly, Charlie," said Commander Joseph ("Red") Flynn, the *Indy*'s second in command. "We're taking water fast. The bow is down. I think we're done for—I recommend we abandon ship."

Flames rose into the sky. Thick smoke poured from the forward deck. There was no power and no lights, save the few emergency lights.

"Commander Flynn, pass the word to abandon ship," McVay ordered. A moment later, Coxswain Keyes rushed to the captain's side.

"Keyes reporting, Captain—I passed the word aft, sir, but I couldn't get forward. There's fire in sick bay and number one mess—I couldn't go any further. Everybody aft is either out or getting out."

The ship lurched to starboard, the list worsening. McVay needed to make sure a distress signal was getting out.

"Lieutenant Orr—see if you can reach the radio room."

"Aye aye, Captain."

McVay shouted below. "Nobody go over the side unless you have a life jacket. She may stay here a minute or two. Get the floater nets against the stack."

To function as a flagship, the *Indianapolis* had been fitted with extra communications equipment to serve the needs of Admiral Spruance's staff. There were two radio shacks, Radio I and Radio II, in rooms about 200 feet from each other. Radioman First Class Joe Moran had gone to Radio I. Also present were watch officer Lieutenant (Junior Grade) Dave Driscoll, Lieutenant Nelson Hill, Radioman Second Class Clifford Sebastian and Radioman Second Class Elwyn Sturtevant. There was smoke from a fire burning in the corner of the room and debris everywhere. Lieutenant Orr arrived from the bridge.

"Get a distress message out right away," he said. "Captain's orders. Say we've been torpedoed and need help immediately."

"The phone to Radio two is dead," Driscoll told him.

"What's the situation?" Hill asked.

"I can't get through to Radio two," Driscoll answered, "and we can't send or receive from here—there's no power." The transmitters were in Radio II. Messages could be sent from Radio I, but the signal had to travel along a wire from Radio I to Radio II, and apparently the explosions had severed the wire somewhere.

"Sturtevant," Hill said. "Go to Radio two and tell Chief Woods to set up on forty-two thirty-five and five hundred kilocycles."

"Aye, sir."

Hill continued. "Moran, you and Sebastian see if you can key from here."

When Sturtevant reached Radio II, where the transmitters were housed, he found it an island of tranquillity in a sea of disorder. Everywhere, smoke billowed and flames poured down passageways as spilled fuel ignited or magazines exploded. Men ran with towels over their heads, scrambled topside, felt their way along darkened corridors, burned their hands on white-hot decks and grabbed for life jackets as the ship slowly rolled over to starboard, but in Radio II, the ventilation was working and the emergency lights were on. Chief Radio Technician Leonard T. Woods was there, accompanied by Jack Miner, who'd been asleep just around the corner in Battle II. Woods knew more about the electronics aboard ship than anyone. Miner noticed that Woods had been burned, but it wasn't slowing him down any.

"We can't reach you from forward," Sturtevant told the chief. "Lieutenant Hill says set up forty-two thirty-five and five hundred. We want to send distress signals."

"The transmitters are already warmed up," Woods replied. "Tell Hill we'll pipe forty-two thirty-five through to him on line three. Bring me a copy of the distress message and we'll key it from here on five hundred."

Sturtevant returned to Radio I. With the power supplied on the line from Radio II, Moran and Sebastian had found that the transmitters in Radio I seemed to be working but the receivers were not, which meant they were unable to monitor their own signals to know for certain if any messages were actually going out. They keyed the message on faith, tapping out in Morse code: USS INDIANAPOLIS . . . TORPEDOED TWICE . . . LATITUDE TWELVE DEGREES NORTH, LONGITUDE ONE HUNDRED THIRTY-FIVE DEGREES EAST . . . NEED IMMEDIATE ASSISTANCE. . . .

"Chief Woods wants a copy of the message," Sturtevant said when he got back to Radio I. "He says he'll send it from there."

Driscoll wrote out the message on a pad of paper and handed it to Radio Technician Second Class Fred Hart.

"Take this to Woods as fast as you can."

Just as Hart left, the ship listed further. A piece of heavy equipment fell from the bulkhead. Driscoll gave an order. "Everyone out—now!"

In Radio II, Chief Radio Technician Woods hadn't waited for anyone from Radio I to return with a copy of the distress message. The radio receiver/transmitter was a large black cabinet filled with vacuum tubes, and though it lacked a transmission key, Woods had jury-rigged a way to send by flipping a toggle switch ordinarily used to test the equipment—he was, in effect, turning the machine on and off to get the signal out. He knew what to say, sending as fast as he could to transmit at 500 kilocycles, the international distress signal frequency: SOS LATITUDE 12 DEGREES NORTH LONGITUDE 135 DEGREES EAST . . .

The signals went out over a powered antenna. Some officers felt the *Indianapolis,* built before the advent of radar, had had enough antennas and other equipment added to her to make her top-heavy and vulnerable. A meter in Radio II measured the power output of the antenna, such that if a signal was being transmitted, the meter fluctuated. Jack Miner watched over Woods's shoulder as the thin red needle on the antenna meter fluctuated. It meant a message was definitely being sent. Miner watched Woods send the message at least three times over a two-minute period. Every radio operator around the world was supposed to monitor 500 kilocycles. The question was, would anybody be paying attention? Then the ship listed even more, and Chief Woods told everyone to get life jackets on and to get out while they still could.

The *Indy* carried two twenty-six-foot-long motorized whaleboats, each designed to carry twenty-two men, and thirty-five life rafts that were supposed to be provisioned with survival gear, including first aid kits, Veery pistols to fire flares called star shells into the sky, signal flags and mirrors, bread in waterproof cans, potable water stored in three-, five- and eight-gallon wooden kegs, several three-and-a-half-pound tins of canned meat called Spam, lanterns, oil, lamp wicks, matches, needles and twine for sail making, tools, fishing reels with line, fishhooks, a hatchet, rifles and ammunition. Because the *Indianapolis* had sailed from Mare Island in such a hurry, not all the rafts were fully provisioned, nor had all the water breakers been refilled with fresh water. Men grappled with the life rafts but managed to free only twelve.

After the first explosion, Mike Kuryla paused on the hangar deck, unsure what to do for a moment, then joined other sailors who were cutting down bundles of kapok life jackets and freeing life rafts. He handed them out as fast as he could, then put one on himself and slid down the ladder to the boat deck as the ship listed. He scrambled to the high side and tried to free one of the whaleboats, pulling at the pins to release it from its davit, but the list was too great. He was hanging on to the lifeline and trying to swing himself over it onto the high side when the ship rolled over on top of him. He took a deep breath, let go of the lifeline and pushed off with his feet, trying to swim out from under it, but the suction was too great. He kicked with all his might, clawing fiercely at the water. He saw his mother's face, and his father's face, and he thought of his brother and of his sister, who'd been sick the last time he'd seen her. He said an act of contrition, thinking he was going to die.

Then he was on the surface, coughing and spitting out black oil. He saw a raft floating in front of him, perhaps one of the ones he'd cut loose with his knife, and climbed into it. A seaman from his crew was already there. There was oil everywhere. He threw up.

"Over here," he called out to anyone who could hear him. "We're over here!"

Morgan Moseley scrambled topside to the galley in his bare feet, wearing only his shorts, saw what was happening and headed below again for his clothes. A friend in the mess hall stopped him and told him he'd better get a life jacket on. He was headed for the galley when the ship listed hard to starboard. He changed his mind and decided the best way topside was through the head, or bathroom. He turned to see a kid behind him, just a boy, probably one of the new recruits. Moseley didn't know the kid's name, but he recognized him because he was always hungry and used to come to the galley to beg for snacks. Moseley told the kid to follow him, then turned the wheel to open the hatch. There was resistance from above. It was stuck.

"We're goners, Moseley, we're goners," the boy said.

"Well, we ain't gone yet, are we?" Moseley replied.

But he couldn't get the hatch open. He thought for a moment that he was going to die. He thought of all the bad things he'd done in his life, how he'd sassed his mother, how he'd stolen a watermelon from a neighbor's watermelon patch. Then the hatch opened. Someone had been standing on the other side of it. He climbed through. He turned to help the kid, but the boy was fumbling with his life jacket. He was a good-looking kid, with black hair and a ruddy complexion. Moseley waited for him. There was fire forward, smoke billowing up from below, the angle of list increasing every second— there was no time to waste, no time to be fumbling with life jackets. The kid was halfway out of the hatch when someone fell from the high side, landed on him and knocked him back down the hole.

The ship rolled. Moseley dove into the water.

• • •

Harlan Twible saw men running everywhere, some partially clothed, some wounded, all of them scared. Commander Flynn told the young ensign to move the men aft. When Twible ran toward the stern, he passed a sailor who was handing out life jackets. The sailor turned out to be one of the men Twible had sentenced, as prosecutor at a captain's mast, to ten days on bread and water in the brig for going AWOL in San Francisco. The ship listed harder to starboard. Perhaps as many as 500 men had gathered aft and were hanging on to anything they could, clustering on the high side, but the stern was rising as the ship went down at the bow. Twible knew men would be injured if it rose any higher. Those who weren't injured from the fall could be crushed if the ship rolled on top of them. If they didn't get into the water immediately, it would be too late.

"Everybody to the low side—now!" Twible yelled. His voice was lost in the din. He repeated his command. "Everybody down the low side—the ship can't be saved." Again, no one heard him, or if they heard him, they were too afraid to obey. He decided to lead by example, shouting, "Everyone follow me!" He worked his way past the cook shack and over the starboard side lifeline. This time, the men followed him.

"Swim away from the ship—as fast as you can! Swim away!"

They swam. Twible turned in time to see the ship disappear, the propellers slowly turning in the air. He found himself in a group of men and asked if anybody had anything floating nearby. A quick survey turned up three life rafts and a couple of floater nets. Twible ordered that the wounded were to be placed in the rafts. Everybody else was to tie himself to a floater net. He had no plan, other than to keep everyone together until the morning. No one else seemed to be taking charge, and as far as he knew, he was the only officer in the group. He'd been trained to lead, so he did. It was as simple as that.

• • •

Gil McCoy released his prisoners from the brig after the second explosion, fumbling for his keys in the dark as the bunk racks all around him collapsed, men falling on top of one another. He found a battery-powered battle lantern to light the compartment. With the help of the two prisoners, he set about pulling men out from under the fallen lockers, bunks and assorted debris, some with broken arms, broken legs, cracked ribs, perhaps as many as thirty men altogether. He'd freed as many as he could from the rubble, maybe twenty, when a chief petty officer stuck his head down from above and shouted through the scuttle, "Dogging the hatch!" McCoy left his lantern behind and ran for the hatch. He was the last man up the ladder, with one more level to go before he made it topside, but he paused, because he knew there were still men trapped below. He could hear them screaming for help, calling out, "Don't leave us!" as the scuttle was closed and secured shut, or "dogged," with steel pins.

He put it out of his mind. He reached the main deck, found a life jacket, climbed to the boat deck on the port side and tried to take his shoes off, but he only had time to untie one of them. As the ship rolled, he walked down the side of the ship and slid off the keel. He swam with all his strength. When he turned around to look, he saw the stern of the ship rise high in the sky above him, men falling off the fantail, getting knocked unconscious as they hit the screws. As the ship went down, the suction pulled him under. He kicked against it. The ship was still exploding as it sank. He felt the concussions. He was finally lifted up by an air bubble, but the suction was strong enough to suck the other shoe off his foot. When he reached the surface, he had to push his way through a gummy mat of oil. He tried to swim underwater to get away from it, but it was everywhere. He swallowed enough of it to make him sick. He saw a raft in the distance and headed for it, but he had trouble pushing through the oil. The raft was drifting farther and farther away. The swim exhausted him. He was losing strength. He managed to grab a rope dangling from the raft, but he was too spent to hang on. Finally somebody grabbed him by the hair and pulled him aboard.

One end of the oval raft had been damaged, but there was enough of a latticed wood floor to give some support. He was coughing and sputtering oil when someone saw the silhouette of a ship, a black shape coursing slowly against the sky. Most of the men in the water feared that the Jap sub had surfaced to strafe the survivors with its machine guns, a tactic practiced by both sides during the war, but McCoy was convinced the ship was a destroyer come to rescue them, so he drew his sidearm and fired two shots, hoping the muzzle flash would attract attention. He was lucky it didn't. There were no U.S. destroyers in the vicinity, but Captain Hashimoto did bring the *I-58* to the surface thirty minutes after the sinking to look for proof of his kill.

Captain McVay was walking upright on the side of his ship as the bow went under, and a wave of water came and washed him into the sea. He swam. He watched as the fantail rose 200 feet in the air. He saw his men jump, and he watched them fall to their deaths. A man falling 100 feet into water might as well be landing on concrete. The *Indianapolis* paused a moment, then slipped into the sea, straight down, picking up speed, with another two miles to fall before she reached the bottom. Men covered in fuel oil wiped their eyes to look for their ship, but there wasn't a ship anymore. They kept looking, but there was only the darkness, the black sky and the endless sea.

It took only twelve minutes. Shorter than halftime at a football game, but enough time to kill about 300 men and put the rest in the water, roughly 880 men scattered 600 miles west of Guam, 550 miles east of Leyte and 250 miles north of the Palau Islands, the closest land.

Twelve minutes.

Chapter Seven

The Ordeal
July 30 to August 3, 1945

Any man unaccustomed to such sights, to have looked over her side that night, would have almost thought the whole round sea was one huge cheese, and those sharks the maggots in it.

Herman Melville, *Moby Dick*

Because the ship kept moving forward as she sank, the distance between the first man to go into the water and the last was about three miles. Men were burned and bleeding, in agony from scorched lungs, broken limbs and cuts, and dazed from cracked skulls and concussions. About half of the 880 men in the water had life jackets, either kapok-filled vests or inflatable rubber belts. A southwesterly current carried them at a speed of about one knot, with winds blowing in about the same direction at an average speed of about five knots, meaning the men would drift about twenty-four miles a day from their initial location. Men in life rafts blew farther in the wind than men submerged in the water because they were more exposed.

• • •

Robert McGuiggan got off the ship near his gun mount, sliding down as the *Indy* dipped forward and rolled to the right at a forty-five-degree angle. He was standing on the keel when he jumped into water covered in a slick of black crude oil, thick and noxious. He swam with his hands in front of him, executing a kind of frantic breaststroke as he tried to clear the muck away. In the darkness he heard a man screaming, "Help me—I can't swim—I don't have a life jacket." McGuiggan turned to help him. The man grabbed him, nearly pulling him under.

"Hang on to my arm," McGuiggan said. "Take it easy—don't panic. I got a rubber life jacket under my kapok." He blew it up and handed it to his shipmate. They saw a group in the water and swam toward it. The group counted about 150 men on the first day. Men formed themselves into circles by tying their life jackets together, comforted by the sense that there would be strength in numbers. Men prayed together, and there was a measure of reassurance in that, as if God were more likely to hear a chorus of petitions than a lone voice in the sea. McGuiggan watched when a sailor swam off to retrieve what looked like a crate of potatoes, maybe sixty feet out, but the sharks got him before he got halfway there, and McGuiggan heard the scream, and decided he wasn't going to look down in the water—if there was something there waiting to take him, he'd rather not see it coming. It was looking down that was making everybody crazy.

Mike Kuryla's group included an ensign and a chief, but no one tried to take charge or tell anybody else what to do. They had about sixteen men sharing four rafts tethered together with about ten feet of line between them, but they had no food and no water. At first they thought they'd be picked up in a matter of hours, but as time wore on, men stopped believing the things they told themselves, and that was when they became suggestible, because they wanted to believe something. Somebody would start hallucinating that they'd found water, fresh, cool, drinkable water, just below the surface. He'd tell another guy and they'd both believe it. Sharks took their victims suddenly, without warning, but there was no way to anticipate it, so all he could do was wait, and hope. It was like a long bad dream, Kuryla thought, one he couldn't wake from. They kept the wounded in the rafts, until they died, and then they turned them loose. Kuryla couldn't believe some of the guys who were hanging on, when other guys who looked like they were in better shape seemed to quit. A fifth of the ship's complement had been new. The younger sailors asked the veteran when he thought they'd be rescued, as if he'd been through something like this before.

"Tomorrow," Kuryla told them. "They'll come and get us tomorrow."

Jack Miner carried with him a similar message of hope. He'd slid into the water with hardly a splash and swam with all his might, fearful that the *Indianapolis* would roll over on top of him. When a bucket struck him from behind, he dove underwater and kicked, holding his breath until he thought his lungs would burst. He surfaced in the middle of a small group of men. He turned in time to see the ship sinking.

"It's gonna be all right," he told the others. "We sent the SOS."

"You sure?" someone asked.

"I'm sure," he said. "It went out. Now all we gotta do is hang on." Seeing the needle move, of course, only told him that the message had been sent. He had no proof that the message had been heard. No listening station had radioed back asking for verification, but wasn't the Pacific Ocean full of guys manning radio sets? Other ships, shore facilities, airfields, pilots in the sky—surely somebody out there had heard the SOS. He saw the needle move.

Morgan Moseley was in the group with Jack Miner. At first he kept to the edge of the circle. He searched from face to face, recognizing no one. It was a large group. He couldn't begin to guess how many men. He thought about the boy in the hatch, the one he'd waited for. He wondered if the boy had managed to get out. He felt guilty for not helping him. He'd tried to help, but he could have tried harder. On the second night in the water, a sailor who couldn't have been more than seventeen told Moseley he was cold and asked if he'd hold him. Moseley agreed. He wasn't going to let another chance to help somebody go by. The two men shared their body warmth and waited for dawn to come. The kid didn't make it. Moseley saw the men around him growing so weak they couldn't hold their heads out of the water, some of them mumbling, "We're all going to die." As far as Moseley was concerned, talking that way made it a kind of self-fulfilling prophecy, so he decided if you could talk yourself into dying, you could just as easily talk yourself into living. He told himself, over and over again, *"I'm not going to die—if anybody is going to live, it's going to be me—I'm going to control my mind. . . ."* It was particularly difficult when they saw airplanes overhead, one flying so low Moseley could read the numbers on the tail. The first impulse was to assume the pilot had seen them. Moseley's hopes soared, then crashed when the passing hours brought no response. One night, he saw the navigation lights of an airplane flying overhead and then, in the distance, miles away, he saw signal flares launched from the sea telling him other men had made it off the ship—surely the plane would see the flares.

• • •

Harlan Twible was more or less in charge of the group that included Jack Miner and Morgan Moseley. He was assessing the situation the morning after the sinking when Lieutenant Redmayne swam over to him and asked him if he was an officer. Twible suggested Redmayne take charge, but the lieutenant was badly burned and said he didn't have enough strength to be of much use. Twible ordered a head count. The count stopped at 325. A quick survey turned up three rafts, provisioned with tins of Spam, malted milk tablets and four casks of fresh water; not much for so many men, but it was better than nothing. Most of the men were covered in oil and unrecognizable. As the sun rose, Twible ordered everyone who wasn't covered in oil to smear some on themselves for protection. He told them to hold on to each other's hands, to stay together. As men died from their injuries during the first day, Twible led or joined in prayer services over their bodies. Most of the men still believed that rescue would come soon. They scanned the horizon, looking for ships or airplanes.

By the second day, men began to hallucinate, seeing ships that weren't there, seeing drinking fountains, islands. Squabbles broke out. Alliances formed. Some men were turning violent. As a precaution, Twible gave the command that everybody disarm. He was backed up by a forty-nine-year-old sea dog, a chief warrant officer named Durward R. "Gunner" Horner, who shouted, "You heard what the officer said." Some did as they were told. Some didn't.

The sharks came in great numbers from all directions that afternoon. Perhaps there were men who'd dropped their knives who wished they still had them, but it wouldn't have made any difference. First one man screamed, then another. The sharks seemed to be attacking the men who'd drifted loose from the nets. The men closed ranks. It didn't help. Men were pulled under, and then their bodies bobbed back to the surface, minus an appendage, only to disappear again. Twible set up shark watches, appointing men to serve as lookouts, but it didn't help much. The sharks periodically came and went, indifferent to both shouts and prayers.

Cozell Smith joined a group of about 150 men hanging on to a floater net. It wasn't much to hang on to, a square rope cargo net about twenty feet to a side, with twelve inches between the ropes and cork floats every two feet. If there was a safe place, it was in the center of the net. The men in the center were less susceptible to shark attack. An ensign was trying to organize the men and get them to move the wounded toward the center, but there were healthy men in the center who wouldn't give up their spots. Everywhere men were screaming. Smith saw shark fins cutting across the surface of the water not ten feet away from him. He saw a man drift from the group, losing consciousness, and then the man jolted as a shark hit him from the side and pulled him under. Men without life jackets tried to climb on top of men with life jackets. Everywhere he looked he saw chaos, as men screamed, panicked, cursed, fought with one another, drowned one another, scrambled over one another like rats in a bucket, the sea black with oil and red with blood. It was, Smith thought, everything he'd ever read about hell.

Suddenly Smith felt a shark take him by the left hand and pull him under before he had a chance to scream. His left hand was in the shark's mouth up to the wrist. He couldn't shake it loose. He could see the shark underwater. It was maybe eight or ten feet long. It rolled, then twisted, trying to rip his hand off. Smith held his breath and pushed at the shark, trying to get his left hand free as the shark jerked from side to side. Smith's right hand slipped off the shark's nose until he felt a soft spot on the side of the shark's head. Smith plunged his middle finger into the soft spot and slid it in all the way to the last knuckle. *His eye,* Smith thought. *I'll rip his eye out if he thinks he can pull me down.* Then the shark turned him loose. Smith kicked for the surface, certain the shark would take him again. He surfaced, gasping for air. His hand was torn and bleeding, but at least it was still connected to his arm. He swam back toward the group, but found he was no longer welcome there. Men feared that Smith's wounds would only attract more sharks.

"Get away!" someone yelled at him.

"Get him!"

"Keep him off—keep him away!"

Gil McCoy was in Kuryla's group, on a different raft, one of four rafts tethered with line. The malted milk tablets only made McCoy thirstier. He tied his T-shirt around his head to keep the sun off, but he got burned all the same. He prayed the rosary repeatedly, using the beads he kept in his pocket. He was the only Catholic in his group, so when the others discovered what he was doing, they asked him to pray out loud so they could learn the words: "Hail Mary, full of grace, the Lord is with thee. . . ." The sharks came, about a dozen, a constant presence. The words of prayer made the idea of dying more bearable, a connection to a world more perfect than this one, more painless and peaceful. It wasn't long before men started losing their minds, saying silly, crazy things. The marine still had his sidearm with him, but after a few hours in the water, the .45 automatic had seized and wouldn't fire. When things started to get nasty as disputes arose, McCoy used the malfunctioning gun to persuade his shipmates to drop their knives. Rank alone carried little authority in the water, but the sight of a .45 conveyed a certain influence.

The sharks, of course, were not so easily bluffed. McCoy thought about his family, his father and his mother and his sisters, but he'd also had two brothers, one who died at birth and another who died at age seven. His main thought was that he didn't want his mother to lose another son. When the thirst or the hunger overwhelmed him, he thought of the pumpkin pies his mother used to bake at Thanksgiving. He was probably the only man in the entire Pacific Ocean thinking of pumpkin pie, but all he wanted was one more piece.

Captain McVay was in a smaller group still. He'd found a potato crate to hold on to at first, then chanced upon two life rafts stacked one atop the other. He climbed into one of the rafts. He'd watched his ship go down in the dim light of a hidden quarter moon, the fantail rising high above his head in ghostly form. He knew the image would be with him forever. He was riding on a greasy film of fuel oil when he heard three men calling for help.

"Over here—I have a raft," he shouted.

He picked up Quartermaster Third Class Vincent Allard, who'd been with him on the bridge as the ship went down. Allard had two younger men with him who were retching and injured. McVay put the two sick men on one of the rafts and tied it to his. He'd been temporarily blinded in one eye by the oil but was otherwise unharmed. His rafts contained paddles, food rations, signal flares and other emergency gear. He knew he'd been lucky to survive the sinking. One of the widely accepted myths about the mariner's life is that a captain is somehow obligated by law or custom or code of honor to go down with his ship. To the contrary, a captain in the United States Navy is commissioned to tend to the safety and well-being of his crew at all times, and would be derelict in his duty if he went down with his ship when there were still members of his crew who could benefit from his guidance.

In the morning, McVay's group hooked up with five men they found hanging on to a raft and a floater net. That made nine men, three rafts and a floater net. McVay ordered a survey of their possessions. They had paddles, biscuits, malted milk tablets, tins of Spam, a single dry cigarette salvaged from a saturated carton that floated by, emergency gear including a Veery pistol and twelve signal cartridges, signal flags and fishing tackle, and a breaker of water. McVay tasted the water and discovered it had gone salty, but he didn't tell the others. He divided the food into rations to last them ten days. He found a pencil and a piece of paper and started a log, drawing up a schedule of two-hour watches for the men to keep, to be sure they didn't miss it if a plane flew overhead. It was a small thing, a pencil and a piece of paper, but it showed leadership at a time when it might have seemed to some that all was lost. It mattered.

Allard made everybody cone-shaped hats from a piece of canvas they found on one of the rafts. McVay, an avid fisherman, attempted to use the fishing gear he found to catch something they could eat. Allard had some luck catching smaller fish, which they used as bait to catch bigger fish, but the sharks that circled the rafts kept stealing the bait. McVay didn't have strong enough tackle to catch a shark. As long as they didn't dangle their legs in the water, his men were relatively safe from sharks, though sharks were known to attack boats and overturn life rafts. To keep their spirits up, they prayed, and they sang songs like "Oh Susanna" and "I'll Be with You in Apple Blossom Time."

The captain sang too. Ordinarily, on a ship, a captain can undermine his own authority by fraternizing too much with his men—he needs to have his orders obeyed immediately by subordinates who regard him as supreme lord and master of the vessel. On his flotilla of life rafts, McVay opened up to them in a way he couldn't have aboard ship. He wanted to know them. He'd lost so many boys whom he'd never known and never would. He asked his men about themselves, where they came from, who was waiting for them back home, what their girlfriends were like, their families. They talked about how hard it was for married men to serve in the navy, constantly away from their wives and loved ones. McVay told them about his second wife, Louise Claytor

McVay, what a great woman she was, a true soul mate, and how she shared his love for duck hunting and fishing. When his men asked him if an SOS had been sent, McVay assured them one had, that he knew it personally. In fact, he'd never heard back from the radio room, so he didn't know whether or not an SOS message had been sent. It was a lie, but if he could set their minds at ease with a white lie, so be it.

They saw planes flying overhead on Monday, most likely bombers leaving from Tinian to bomb the Japanese home islands, and tried to signal to them with mirrors and yellow signal flags, to no avail. McVay saw a raft in the distance that day, bobbing on the waves about a mile off, occupied by a lone sailor. They saw him again Tuesday morning and paddled over to him, a four-and-a-half-hour exercise that left everybody spent. It turned out he was just a kid, barely old enough to serve, scared and alone, his face black with oil. It made the captain feel good to bring him into the group, which now consisted of ten men and four rafts. He pointed out to the others that the *Indianapolis* had been due to arrive in Leyte this morning, and that when they didn't show up, a search would surely be ordered.

At least that was the way it was supposed to work.

In a general sense, what the men in the water were experiencing was beyond their comprehension, a lesson of pain and suffering that made its impression as much on their minds as on their bodies. The first to die in the water were those who drowned or succumbed to injuries suffered aboard ship. Most of them were burn victims. In the early hours of the ordeal, the injured men slowly bled out, went into shock and died from exsanguination. Before the bodies were set adrift, they were searched for dog tags or personal effects to be forwarded to the next of kin. Not everyone made it off the ship with identification on them.

Many of the men who didn't die of burns or injuries suffered during the sinking died from exposure. "Exposure" (sometimes the word "immersion" was used) was a kind of catchall term to describe a variety of maladies and afflictions, each terrible in its own way. When experienced together, they proved a deadly combination. First, there was the water itself. Salt water is corrosive to human skin and can cause saltwater ulcers, a condition affecting the parts of the body that remain above the water, where grains of sodium chloride deposited on the skin through evaporation get ground into the epidermis by abrasion or chafing—a life preserver strap rubbing against the neck, for instance—causing microscopic cuts that then become infected. Next, there was the sun to contend with. At midday, in midsummer, a mere twelve degrees from the equator, the sun is fierce, pushing the temperatures over 100 degrees. Ultraviolet light doesn't penetrate seawater beyond a few feet, but all the same, the sun glaring off the surface of the water burned men's faces and necks. Severely sunburned skin coming in contact with salt water can feel like you've been splashed with acid. Second-degree sunburns were accompanied by blistering. Sunburned ulcers would have been excruciating.

Those men who were covered in fuel oil found themselves grateful for it, despite the vomiting and nausea caused by the fumes, because the oil coating protected them from the sun's ultraviolet rays—protected everything, that is, except their eyes. Without shade or protection, and with white-hot sunlight refracting and reflecting off every wave and facet of the ocean's surface, many men suffered from "photophobia" or sunburned corneas, where the eyes become hypersensitive and any exposure to light hurts. Some men tied their shirts around their eyes as blindfolds, while others covered their eyes with their hands or arms and waited for night to come.

Because the body can survive for weeks without food by metabolizing its own energy reserves, first fat and then muscle tissues, starvation was not much of a problem. Emotionally, hunger could have contributed to a feeling of despondency or listlessness or a lack of benevolence toward one's fellow man. Food would also have helped combat the effects of hypothermia, a far more immediate threat than malnutrition.

Hypothermia describes a condition in which the body's temperature drops because of exposure to cold. Water has to reach ninety-five degrees before it's considered thermally neutral, the point at which heat lost from the body is balanced by heat produced by the body's metabolism. Even in the tropics, the water doesn't get that warm. The midday sun would only have heated the water near the surface. Water from the chest down would have remained cold. Because air is a poorer conductor of heat than water, those men in life rafts who were able to stay dry were less likely to suffer from hypothermia than men who remained submerged.

Hypothermia can kill, once the body's core temperature drops below eighty-eight degrees, but for the men of the *Indianapolis,* it had a more insidious effect. When the body senses its core temperature dropping, it restricts the flow of blood to the extremities, but that blood has nowhere else to go, and as a result, the body's core fills up with fluids. The brain senses the buildup of excess fluids in the core and directs the body to get rid of them through urination—why waste energy keeping urine warm when you can just expel it? The result is dehydration.

Few of the men who went into the water after the ship sank had anything with them to drink. The men with severe burns would have become dehydrated from their injuries, since the chief function of the skin is to keep fluids in and everything else out, and fluids leak out where the skin is damaged. Third-degree burns ooze lymph fluid, a yellowish substance that is essentially blood without the red blood cells. Lymph fluids can in some cases dry to form a seal over a burn wound, but they won't do that in water.

The pressure of the water alone can cause dehydration because

water pressure increases as depth increases. The pressure a man tread-
ing water feels below his waist is greater than the pressure he feels above
the waist. That pressure squeezes the blood from the legs and forces it
back up into the torso, where once again the brain senses excess fluid
levels in the core. It's the same reason some people feel the urge to uri-
nate when they swim in a lake or a swimming pool.

Without fresh water to drink, the survivors experienced unimag-
inable thirst. First your mouth turns to cotton. Your saliva turns thick and
bitter, until it disappears altogether. You become aware of your tongue as
a fat dry thing barricading your air passage. Your throat dries out until
you can't talk, and you feel a massive lump in your windpipe, forcing you
to swallow again and again, and every swallow is painful, but the lump
won't go away. Without tears in your tear ducts, your eyelids begin to
crack, and you might weep blood. The lump in your throat grows as your
air passage swells up, until you feel like you're drowning. You can't
breathe. The sun cracks your lips, but passing your tongue over them
does no good. The skin around your mouth and nose pulls back and
shrivels. Your lungs rattle when you inhale. Severe dehydration feels like
every cell in your body is crying out for water, largely because every cell in
your body truly is. All the normal metabolic processes continue to function as best they can, each cell taking in oxygen and metabolizing it to
produce waste products, which the body then has to get rid of by producing urine in the kidneys. Without an intake of fresh water, the body
essentially begins to drink from itself. It wouldn't help for a man to be
overweight because there's very little water in fat. The kidneys have to
keep functioning to flush the toxins in the body, so they take water from
wherever they can find it.

The cellular craving for water affects the mind as well. The cells
in the brain need water to function just like any other cell in the body.
Mineral deficiencies and chemical imbalances created by the buildup of
toxins and waste products short-circuit the electrical activity in the

brain and can cause hallucinations at worst and poor judgment at best, a lack of reason or temporary insanity. The men in the water suffered a variety of delusions. Some believed that the water at their feet had to be fresh water because it was colder than the water nearer the surface, and that it would be safe to dive down and take a drink, as long as the water they drank was cold. Others came to believe that the *Indianapolis* had sunk in a very shallow place in the ocean and that she was just a few feet below them, with plenty of fresh water still on board for anybody who wanted to dive down and get it. Many believed they saw sources of water in the distance, islands with streams and waterfalls, even hula girls in grass skirts offering them cool drinks. Still others believed they could hold seawater in their cupped hands for a few minutes until the salt evaporated and they could drink what remained, when in fact just the opposite was true—the water in their hands would become saltier as the potable water evaporated. Some men thought they could just hold a little water in their mouths without swallowing it, and that maybe that would satisfy them. As one day turned to two, then three, then four, many found it harder and harder to resist, until they finally succumbed to the temptation and took deep drafts of salt water, expecting a great quenching and blessed relief.

They couldn't have been more wrong. The result of drinking salt water is hypernatremia, an excess of salt in the body. It's something like pouring gasoline on a fire to put it out, because a dehydrated body is already having a difficult time ridding itself of toxins, and salt is a toxin. Imbibing seawater dramatically increases the amount of toxins the body has to expel, forcing the kidneys to extract additional water from the fluids around the cells and from the cells themselves. Hypernatremia can damage nerves and cell membranes and cause severe muscle cramps, intestinal cramps and convulsions, as well as neurological problems and hallucinations. Men who drank salt water died extremely uncomfortable deaths. How long it took depended on how much they drank, but death was virtually guaranteed once they imbibed the poison.

Many of the men went "out of their heads," to varying degrees, for varying lengths of time, from simple sleep deprivation. Hallucinations, compelling fantasies, obsessive thoughts, uncontrollable fears and emotions, delirium, hopelessness and despair are all expressions of psychic damage, and during sleep is the time when the psyche heals and repairs itself by dreaming. Without sleep, microscopic psychic injuries can rub and chafe and become infected too.

It's not just any kind of sleep that the mind needs to repair itself. The deepest sleep we experience, perhaps a dozen times a night, is called Rapid Eye Movement, or REM, sleep. It's also the time when our muscles become totally relaxed, to the point where we can no longer move. REM sleep is absolutely essential to our well-being. In a pioneering study of REM sleep done at Stanford University, rats were deprived of REM sleep when they were placed on an overturned flowerpot in the middle of a bucket of water. The rat being studied could balance on the pot as long as it had muscle tone, even fall asleep, but as soon as it entered REM and lost muscle tone, it fell off the pot and into the water. After a few days, the formerly docile laboratory rats turned into hyperaggressive, psychotic rats that fought with one another and bit the lab workers who were trying to handle them. What happened to the men in the water was similar to what happened to those rats. The men wearing life jackets who tried to sleep found that as soon as they lost muscle tone, their faces would fall forward into the water, waking them up and depriving them of REM sleep.

When men could doze off (and never for more than a few minutes at a time) they experienced a much lighter, less restorative kind of sleep called hypnagogic sleep. Whereas REM sleep brings with it dreams unrelated to current experience or daily life, hypnagogic dreams at the onset of sleep take place in the borderland between sleep and wakefulness, and correspond more closely to recent events in the subject's life, fusing reality and fantasy. Hypnagogic dreams tend to be primarily visual in quality, hallucinations that seem, to the dreamer, to be quite well organized and internally coherent, bizarre fantasies that nevertheless make perfect sense somehow. They are also dreams we feel we can participate in rather than simply observe. Hypnagogic dreams also tend to express a heightened awareness of the body's position or condition, dreams where, for example, if your arm has fallen asleep in bed, you might dream your hand has become encased in concrete and you can't lift it.

No wonder, then, that men saw islands in the distance, or hula girls in grass skirts and coconut bikinis offering them tall, frosty glasses of lemonade. Little wonder either that so many survivors seemed to share their hallucinations or hold delusional thoughts in common, because in a hypnagogic state, suspended in the borderland halfway between sleep and wakefulness, a man is also extremely suggestible, which explains how when one man hallucinated and said he saw an island in the distance, or a hula girl, or a ship, other men agreed and said they saw them too. It also explains why, when one man shouted out, in fear and anguish, "Jap! This guy's a Jap—kill him!" other men picked up the cry and used their knives to protect themselves or to avenge the deaths of their shipmates. Some men broke. Some didn't. Some stayed in control of themselves and some lost control. Many men found strength in their religious faith. Some men found strength in their families and loved ones, living for the wives or the children or the girlfriends they had left behind, even living because they knew how sad their siblings would be or how disappointed their parents would be in them if they didn't.

Men who didn't die from burns, injuries or exposure died from shark attacks; it's impossible to estimate how many. They were scattered across the sea over a distance of about twenty miles, out of sight from one another, many dying alone and unaccounted for. Some survivors never saw sharks. Others saw them in great numbers. By the first morning, men saw fins breaking the surface, circling them. Men tipped their heads forward and gazed into the waters, where they saw large groups of sharks swarming beneath their feet, as far down as the light penetrated.

It's also impossible to estimate the total number of sharks on the scene, but it is possible to guess the type. Some survivors reported seeing fins "white as a sheet of paper," indicating the presence of oceanic whitetips (*Carcharhinus longimanus*). Blue sharks (*Prionace glauca*), one of the widest-ranging of all sharks, would also have inhabited the area, recognizable by their pointed snouts, long narrow pointed pectoral fins and slender bodies. Silky sharks would have been present as well. Both whitetips and blues are known to be dangerous to humans.

Sharks arriving on the scene to investigate would have found a number of things telling them that prey was about. First, as opportunistic predators, sharks seek out prey that is the least likely to flee or fight back. In the ocean, sharks will look for injured fish before they look for non-injured fish. To do that, they have extremely sensitive hearing and specialized organs along their lateral lines and on their snouts. Consequently, although splashing and kicking in the water was a strategy some survivors deployed to drive sharks off, it may have had the opposite effect of drawing them closer by imitating the sounds and motions of a wounded fish.

Sharks also possess an acute sense of smell, able to detect minute amounts of organic material in seawater and follow those trace elements back to their source. Blood is one of those organic materials, detectable by sharks at as little as one part blood per 1,000,000 parts seawater. Survivors who pushed away the wounded from their midst, figuring the blood from their wounds was attracting sharks, were essentially correct. Blood was not, however, the only thing attracting sharks. Urine did too, and survivors who weren't bleeding were involuntarily discharging urine as dehydration increased, in which case the strategy of pushing away the wounded had no effect. Sharks would also have been attracted by the vomit in the water. Once at close range, sharks would have used their eyes to zero in on their prey, as well as organs located at the front of their heads called ampullae of Lorenzini, which detect the minute electrical fields given off by all living things. In effect, any shark investigating the explosions that night would have been virtually overloaded with sensory information telling him a substantial feeding opportunity had presented itself. For the men in the water, playing dead made no difference. Men in groups were marginally safer than men who found themselves alone in the sea, but no one was truly safe. The first bite of a shark would have been comparatively gentle, as the predator mouthed its prey, testing to see if it contained sufficient nutritional value. The second and third bites were the ones that killed.

By the second day, Lieutenant Redmayne was feeling better and made an effort to establish order. Twible welcomed the help. He'd begun to feel himself weakening, and turned increasingly to prayer. He never felt like he was going to die, and he'd been too busy to hallucinate, but he was so tired. Perhaps the navy had let him down, but he knew that God would not. He thought of his brothers, and of his kid sister, Joyce, who at fifteen was still living at home with their parents. Some of the men in the water weren't much older than Joyce, boys who'd gotten their parents' permission to join at seventeen. It didn't take long for Twible to feel like he was no longer a green ensign fresh out of the academy. He thought of his wife, Alice. He thought of the words to the navy hymn he'd learned at Annapolis: *"Oh hear us when we cry to thee for those in peril on the sea. . . ."*

Around him, he saw men barely able to hold their own heads up who were still trying to help their shipmates, speaking words of encouragement that perhaps they themselves did not believe. He saw men risk shark attacks by swimming out to retrieve a shipmate who'd drifted off or lost his mind chasing hallucinations. He also discovered men who were hoarding rations, two rafts where a rebel contingent ate Spam and malted milk tablets without regard for the others. Twible was outraged, and suggested to Redmayne that they had to be stopped. Redmayne did his best, identifying himself as the senior officer in the group and ordering the hoarders to turn their rations over to him for safekeeping and equitable distribution—a few swam over to Redmayne's raft and obeyed him, but the majority did not. Twible feared the rebel actions would harm discipline and knew they might attack him with their knives, even kill him, but he wasn't afraid of them when he swam to the rebel rafts, saw the provisions they'd stashed away and shouted, "Give it all back!" When his command was ignored, he reached in and physically seized the food and water, first from one raft, then the other, removing them to Redmayne's command raft.

The next day, Wednesday, there was a new uprising as four men, joined by Ensign Blum, decided they wanted to take one of the rafts and some of the provisions and try to paddle to the island of Yap, several hundred miles to the south. It was a lunatic idea, but Redmayne put it to a vote and the raft was allowed to leave. Until Blum came forward, Redmayne and Twible had assumed they were the only officers in the group. The raft set off, the men in it paddling only a few hundred yards before exhaustion set in. The men who stayed behind weakened and died in increasing numbers that night.

Jack Miner didn't much care for Lieutenant Redmayne's interference after he'd ordered Miner out of a raft, even though it was Miner's turn to rest. Why was this idiot officer trying to tell people what to do? It was true that things were deteriorating rapidly. Vicious fights had broken out. Men used their knives against one another. Maybe Redmayne was just trying to get control of the situation, but it seemed like he was commandeering a raft for his own personal use. He was screaming, "Get off the raft—off the raft and into the water—get away from the raft!" He was just making things worse.

Miner vowed to himself, *If I ever get Redmayne alone, I'm going to beat him to death.*

Some who agreed with Miner's sentiments were mollified when Redmayne drank a small amount of salt water and went out of his head and Twible had to crack him over the head with a tin of malt tablets, knocking him out, an act that may have saved Redmayne's life. Miner was sad, not angry, when his friend Ray died in his arms. The kid had just gotten engaged in Vallejo. He'd shown everybody the ring. Miner had even met the guy's fiancée before they sailed from San Francisco, a real nice gal. Ray was going to be happy. It was all laid out for him. Then he died. Miner just couldn't hold him anymore, and Ray wasn't trying to save himself. He was saying crazy things, really tormented. Miner tried to hold him up, but he couldn't do it.

Morgan Moseley heard Redmayne and Twible giving orders, but mainly, he was just trying to mind his own business and avoid the insanity all around him.

"Hey, Moseley," a shipmate said to him on the third day. "Guess where I was last night? I went home. I'm going home again tonight and I asked my wife and she told me it would be all right if I brought you home with me to stay in the guest room. What do you think?"

Moseley knew the guy was bananas, but to the kid, what he was saying was entirely real. Moseley declined the offer, but he couldn't judge the guy, because he'd had something of a vision himself—he'd seen the inside of a motel room, right in front of him, maybe ten or twenty feet off, with a single bed in the middle, the covers pulled back invitingly. He shook his head, but the vision didn't go away. He was so thirsty his teeth were coming loose. He tried to pass his tongue over them, but his tongue was swollen to twice its size. The men around him were drinking salt water, but Moseley had the sense to know they would soon be gone.

On Wednesday night, the fighting worsened, men cursing and scratching, wielding their knives, but it wasn't happening anywhere near him, and he didn't turn to look, and there was nothing he could have done about it anyway. Everything felt hazy, dreamlike, confusing and unclear, until he knew he was in a group of men in the water somewhere, but that was about it. He didn't want to die, but he didn't much care one way or the other—he could feel his ability to reason slipping away. Then, somehow, he came out of it on his own when a small group of sailors, three or four men, approached him and asked him if he wanted to come with them—they were swimming to a nearby island. He knew they wouldn't get 100 yards. When he looked in the water below him, he saw a swarm of sharks clearly enough to distinguish between the different types, sharks of two or three different colors, idly circling. He decided not to swim to the nonexistent nearby island.

Maurice Bell thought of his wife, Lois. He remembered how he and his buddies had gone into the restaurant where she worked and ordered as many glasses of water as they could, just to see how many she'd bring before she said anything. Sixteen glasses of water on the table. Imagine that. What he wouldn't give now for sixteen glasses of water.

Mike Kuryla's group of four rafts had been spared the kind of fighting that afflicted some of the other groups, but that didn't mean they weren't feeling desperate. On the morning of the fourth day, Thursday, the decision was made to split up, with one raft heading north, one south, one east and one west in search of shipping lanes and possible rescue. It seemed like a foolish idea to Kuryla—surely the more of them who stayed together, the greater their chances of being spotted from the air. Then again, he understood the desire to do something rather than just sit and wait.

By Thursday, there were five men still alive on Gil McCoy's broken raft. The only other survivor still conscious was Gunner's Mate Bob Brundige, from Des Moines, Iowa. McCoy was glad of the company. He wasn't telling himself he was going to make it anymore. He just wanted to make sure that when he died, he did it right. He'd almost died when a shark stuck his head through a hole in the bottom of the raft, but McCoy had managed to kick the shark in the eye and send it spiraling off in what he hoped was pain. There were other sharks, and he wouldn't be able to fight them off forever.

"When I'm the last guy left," McCoy told Brundige, "I just want you to know I'll take care of you guys for as long as I can."

"What makes you so sure you're going to be the last guy alive?" Brundige asked.

"Because I'm a marine," he joked. "I'm tougher than hell."

"I'm an Iowa farmer," Brundige replied. "That makes me a whole lot tougher than you."

McCoy smiled.

Later that afternoon, he wasn't sure if he was out of his head or not. If he were, he'd probably be the last to know, but suddenly it became important to him to scrub the oil from his body. When he'd served as Captain McVay's orderly, he always made sure his shoes were shined and his uniform was clean and pressed. He'd always taken pride in his appearance, and if he was going to meet his maker in the near future, he certainly didn't want to be standing at the gates of heaven looking like a rag somebody'd used to clean a jeep engine. The water around the raft was clear of oil by now, so he jumped in and started scrubbing, despite the fact that the sharks were still circling.

"What are you doing?" Brundige asked him.

"What's it look like?" he replied. "I'm not going to heaven covered in oil."

"Get back in the raft," Brundige advised.

McCoy eventually did, but he'd reached the point where he knew dying would be a lot easier than living. He even cupped his hands and brought a small amount of salt water to his lips, tapped it with the tip of his tongue, tasted the brine and considered. Wasn't he a marine? Weren't marines tough? Tough enough to drink salt water? *Now you're nuts,* he thought. *You gotta stop thinking like that—that's crazy.* He thought again of his mother, how much he loved her, how sad she'd be if she lost him—he couldn't let that happen to her. He thought as well of how proud he was to be a marine, and how he had to hang on for the sake of the corps, and he let the water trickle through his fingers.

Cozell Smith found himself at the center of the worst kind of madness, his own internal insanity matched to a perception that everyone around him was crazy too. He couldn't trust anyone; many of the men around him had reverted to their basest natures. He watched as one man started screaming, "Jap! This guy's a Jap—kill him!" Soon several others set upon the unfortunate sailor who'd been declared a Jap and together they managed to drown him, even though Smith knew the man was a shipmate and not a Jap. Smith felt helpless to stop any of it.

Then it got worse. He witnessed men committing acts of cannibalism. It all seemed like a series of hallucinations, but if that were true, he wasn't the only one seeing things. Others saw things too. Smith saw a man use his knife to cut at the wrist of a dead body, apparently thinking nobody else was watching, but Smith could see everything. The ocean swells only partially obscured his view. The water rose and fell, like a curtain opening and closing. Smith tried to close his eyes, terrified at what he might see.

"Look," someone else said. "He's eating that arm." Elsewhere, a sailor humped over the body of a dead man, drinking blood from a cut he'd made in the corpse's throat. At least that was what it looked like. It didn't matter if it really happened or if it was just another manifestation of collective delusion—Smith experienced it as real, the image burned forever into his memory.

Compared to the others, Captain McVay's group was in good shape. Sharing four rafts among eleven men reduced the group's exposure to hypothermia and dehydration by keeping them out of the water. The rafts also afforded them the opportunity to sleep. As a result, none suffered from psychotic episodes or hallucinations. In addition, where in other groupings ensigns and lieutenants were having trouble keeping order, no one in McVay's group questioned their captain's authority, and that provided stability and discipline. All the same, they felt hopeless, despairing that rescue would ever come. Their captain had told them SOSs had gone out. Why, then, hadn't anybody come looking for them? It made no sense.

Chapter Eight

The Rescue
August 2 to 3, 1945

Are we men—grown men—salt sea men—men nursed upon dangers and cradled in storms—men made in the image of God and ready to do when He commands and die when He calls. . . . I don't know where this ship is, but she's in the hands of God, and that's good enough for me. . . . If it is God's will that we pull through, we pull through—otherwise not.

Mark Twain, *The Great Dark*

Rescue came somewhat by accident on Thursday when a pilot named Lieutenant Wilbur C. ("Chuck") Gwinn thought he saw something in the water. He was flying at 3,000 feet in a Lockheed Ventura PV-1 bomber, on a routine patrol mission. They were out over the ocean when a newly repaired antenna broke again. Gwinn turned the controls over to his copilot and headed for the tail of the plane to see if he could fix it himself. There was an opening in the tail of the aircraft, a gunner's hatch where Gwinn crouched to see the wire antenna whipping wildly in the wash behind the plane. He'd just ordered his machinist's mate to reel in the antenna, figuring he'd tie a piece of rubber hose to the end to stabilize it, when he looked down and saw an oil slick spread out across the sea. An oil slick often meant a Japanese submarine below. He ordered his bomb bay doors opened, his depth charges armed, then took control of the airplane, diving to 150 feet. He was just about to drop his bombs when he saw tiny bumps in the slick and realized they were men, stranded in the middle of nowhere. He had no idea if they were Americans or perhaps Japanese submariners. He hadn't been told of any ships sunk in the area, and agreed with the others who considered this part of the Pacific to be the backwaters of the war, far from any significant action.

He circled back, deciding that whoever they were, Americans or Japanese, he would help them, and dropped a life raft, kegs of water and a sonobuoy. This high-tech floating sound-detection device was meant to pick up enemy submarine sounds and radio them back to the airplane, but it was possible to send voice messages over it. The sonobuoy didn't work, and the kegs of water ruptured when they hit the surface of the ocean. Gwinn sent an urgent message to squadron headquarters at 11:25 A.M. that read: SIGHTED 30 SURVIVORS 011–30 NORTH 133–30 EAST. DROPPED TRANSMITTER AND LIFEBOAT EMERGENCY IFF ON 133–30. Turning to the northeast, he followed the oil slick and saw more bumps in the sea, a total of 150. From this he knew they weren't Japanese submariners, because Japanese subs didn't carry that many men. They had to be Americans, but where had they come from? He dropped all the supplies he had, then hurried back to the tail of the plane to reel in the antenna. He tied the piece of rubber hose to the end and let it back out, hoping it would work properly now, and ordered his radioman to send a revised message. SEND RESCUE SHIP 11–15N 133–47E 150 SURVIVORS IN LIFEBOATS AND JACKETS. . . .

For a pilot to see a human head in the water, he has to be looking straight down, and unless a pilot is banking sharply, he's usually looking down at about a thirty-degree angle. Seeing a man in the water would be as difficult as seeing the dot at the end of this sentence projected onto a movie screen in a theater from the back row. In the end, it was the oil slick that saved them.

Gwinn's message got through to his base on the island of Peleliu. Gwinn's superior, Lieutenant Commander George Atteberry, heard the first message and immediately drove over to squadron VPB-23, which flew PBY-5A Catalina seaplanes, squat, chunky, amphibious aircraft that commonly went by the nickname of Dumbo, named after a popular cartoon elephant. Dumbos were used primarily to drop rescue gear to downed pilots or shipwrecked sailors. Two of the three Catalinas in the squadron were already flying missions, but one, code-named *Playmate 2,* was on standby. The pilot was Lieutenant Robert Adrian Marks, 28, who'd become a navy flyer in 1942. His crew loaded their aircraft with 1,250 gallons of fuel (enough to stay airborne for twelve hours), flares, life rafts, dye markers and shipwreck kits and headed out at 12:40 P.M. for what would be about a three-hour flight at the Dumbo's top speed of 100 knots.

Atteberry took off right behind Marks in a second Ventura, a much faster plane than the Catalina, hoping to reach the scene ahead of the Dumbo to relieve Gwinn, who would be running out of fuel soon. Atteberry reached the scene at 2:15 and was shocked to find so many men in the water, radioing back to Peleliu to confirm that there were at least 150. Marks overheard Atteberry's report. At 2:30, still on his way north, Marks flew over a destroyer escort, the USS *Cecil J. Doyle,* whose captain, Lieutenant Commander W. Graham Claytor, called Marks up on the radio and asked him where he was going. Marks told him. Claytor turned the *Doyle* around and steamed north at flank speed before receiving orders to do so, a violation of protocol and a potentially punishable offense. But if there were men in the water, Claytor knew that wasted minutes could cost lives, and there was no telling how long it would take for the orders to divert to come through.

Other ships were soon ordered to the scene, including the *Dufilho,* the *Bassett,* the *Ringness,* the *Register,* the *Ralph Talbot* and the *Madison,* all within 200 miles of the disaster. Lieutenant Marks arrived on site at 3:50 P.M. and flew low over the area where men were strewn in the sea on a roughly north-south axis. He dropped rafts, dye markers, emergency rations and shipwreck kits. He radioed back to base at 4:25, without even bothering to put his message in coded form: BETWEEN 100 AND 200 SURVIVORS AT POSITION REPORTED. NEED ALL SURVIVAL EQUIPMENT AVAILABLE WHILE DAYLIGHT HOLDS. MANY SURVIVORS WITHOUT RAFTS. At 4:30, he added to his previous message, saying, WILL ATTEMPT OPEN SEA LANDING.

He was informing, not asking permission. Marks made his decision to land because as he circled low, he'd actually seen sharks taking men in the water, and the sight horrified him. There was a standing order in the squadron that nobody was allowed to land PBY-5As in open water. Unlike the standard PBYs, PBY-5As had three large wheels, which, though retractable, put extra weight in the nose and made the aircraft less seaworthy. Other attempts to land 5As in the open water had met with disaster, but Marks decided it was worth the risk, and when he polled his crew to ask them what they thought, they agreed. He'd established a reputation for fearlessness in prior rescues, and his men admired him for that. The wind was eight knots, blowing from the north, but the seas contained twelve-foot swells running from the northwest, promising a roller-coaster landing at best. At worst, *Playmate 2* could break up if it hit the sea wrong. Insofar as he was putting his crew in danger, Marks was aware that he could be court-martialed later, but right now, men were being ripped to pieces by sharks.

The plane bounced fifteen feet in the air the first time it hit the water, bounced twice more and settled in. It had popped some rivets and cracked at the seams, slowly taking on water, but for the most part, it had held. Marks taxied, looking for men to pull out of the water. He steered clear of men in larger groups, calculating that the loners and the single swimmers needed him more, though it was heartbreaking to pass anyone by. One of his crewmen was an ensign named Morgan Hensley who'd been an amateur wrestler and possessed great upper-body strength. Hensley leaned out the portside blister and plucked men from the sea like they were soggy rag dolls. The plane was carrying eighteen gallons of fresh water in four breakers. The crew gave each man they hauled aboard half a cup of water, waited a few minutes and then administered half a cup more. When the fuselage of the PBY-5A was filled to capacity, Marks's crew began putting men on the wings, tying them in place with parachute shrouds so that they wouldn't fall back into the rolling sea. By the time darkness came, Marks had rescued fifty-six men—fifty-six skeletons, smelling of oil and vomit and urine, crying softly in pain but alive.

Another PBY landed. More planes arrived, circling overhead, dropping gear. Surface ships closed in from all directions. The first to arrive was the *Doyle*. Captain Claytor had been in radio contact with Marks, knew how desperate the situation was and sailed at flank speed, reaching the scene shortly after dark. He immediately ordered his crew to sweep the sea with one of two 24-inch searchlights. Around 9:00 P.M., he made a decision and ordered his other searchlight pointed straight up in the sky, casting a beam that was visible for 60 miles and throwing a pale pinkish glow on the clouds 2,000 feet overhead. His beam would also have been visible to any Japanese submarine, ship or airplane within 60 miles, and he was therefore putting his own crew at risk and himself in jeopardy of court-martial. In Claytor's judgment, it was more important that the men still in the sea, however many there were, wherever they were, be given a signal that help was at hand. As other surface ships arrived, they turned on their searchlights as well, sending out whaleboats and landing craft to collect the men in the water without further delay.

• • •

For McGuiggan, rescue began when a B-17 flew over in the late afternoon and dropped a life raft. He'd lost track of time and thought it was still the second day. McGuiggan summoned the last of his strength and swam for the raft. At the raft, he met a shipmate from Indiana, a man named Hamer Campbell who'd come from another group. Picking Campbell out of the water, McGuiggan looked down for the first time and saw sharks, layers of them. Only when they paddled back to McGuiggan's original group did he realize that what had started out to be 150 men was now down to about 15. Everyone got into the raft. It was cold. McGuiggan passed out. Finally they saw a searchlight in the distance illuminating the clouds. They paddled toward it. He passed out again, or slept—what was the difference? He awoke early in the morning, and had to prop his eyelids open with his fingers because they'd crusted over with ulcers. He saw a ship coming closer. Men on the ship started shooting at him. What was this? More Japs? In fact the rescue ship had sent a swimmer to the raft with a lifeline to tie to it. The men on the ship weren't shooting at the men in the raft—they were shooting at the sharks surrounding the swimmer. McGuiggan was brought aboard the USS *Talbot* and later transferred to the USS *Register*.

Mike Kuryla never saw Chuck Gwinn's airplane or the subsequent landing of Adrian Marks. Later he saw planes dropping survival gear into the water, but he was too spent to care. His roller-skating buddy Paul saw it too and left the group to swim for a package that splashed down a few hundred yards off. It was the last Kuryla ever saw of his friend. Kuryla was finally rescued when the USS *Register* sent a Higgins boat, a flat-bottomed plywood landing craft manned by sailors with rifles, which they fired at the sharks in the water to drive them off. When the sailors hauled Kuryla aboard, all he could say was, "What took you so long?"

• • •

Jack Miner saw a seaplane land in the distance on Thursday afternoon. It was too far away to swim to, but it was good that somebody
had arrived, finally, at last. Maybe there were other guys still alive. He
rode the waves, scanning the horizon when he was at the crest of a wave,
but he couldn't see very far. He got angry when he realized how long it
had taken the navy to send somebody. He saw the seaplane again—
maybe that was all they were going to send, one little plane. They were
making a mess of it. He waited. Night came. He thought they were never
going to find him. He got on a raft. There were a few other guys on the
raft with him. In the wee hours of the morning, he saw a searchlight, a
small craft, coming toward him.

"Japs," he shouted. "They're coming for us—everybody get
out! Kick!"

He was trying to swim away when he felt a hand on his arm and
a sailor lifted him out of the sea. He was brought aboard the USS *Bassett*.

Morgan Moseley saw the lights of the *Doyle* illuminating the sky.
The ship was far away, little more than a shape on the horizon, but the distance wasn't enough to deter several of his shipmates who decided they
were going to swim to the ship. They got about fifty feet and started yelling
for help, but no one had the strength to go to them. Their calls for help
soon ceased. Moseley waited. Around four in the morning, he saw a searchlight approaching, sweeping the water. A ship. A cargo net was lowered
over the side. He grabbed on and was hauled on board. He couldn't stand
up. Someone cut his clothes off him. He'd weighed 205 pounds when he
went into the water and 160 when he came out. Someone gave him orange
juice. Someone said, "You must be feeling awfully good about now."

"It would have been nicer," he wanted to say, "if you'd come a little sooner."

Harlan Twible saw the airplanes circling, though he was beginning to doubt his own sanity. One dropped a lifeboat, which Twible swam to. The boat contained cans of water and cigarettes, which he passed around. A short time later, Adrian Marks landed his PBY a few hundred yards off. Several of the men from the group decided they would swim to the plane. Twible tried to order them to stop, arguing that it was safer to stay put and wait, but they wouldn't listen. Among those swimming for the plane was yet another officer who'd chosen to conceal his rank, an ensign named Tom Brophy who came from a wealthy family. Brophy drowned in the attempt, one of the last to die in the water.

When a whaleboat from the USS *Bassett* finally pulled Harlan Twible out of the water, the fit 154-pound Annapolis graduate had been reduced to a 129-pound invalid. One sailor on the boat held him while the other cut him out of his life jacket. When the whaleboat reached the *Bassett,* the two sailors carried Twible up the ladder with great tenderness. Twible wobbled on his feet, held by a man on each side, as he saluted the officer of the deck and reported in, "We are the crew of the USS *Indianapolis,* sir." He'd taken some shrapnel in his side when the torpedo hit, so his wounds were bandaged, and he was given a transfusion as well as water. He thanked God that he was safe and alive. Of the 325 men who had been in his group the first morning, only 171 remained.

Cozell Smith saw a plane circling overhead. It circled for a long time, flying low over the water. Finally it dropped a package into the water, about 300 yards off. He wondered whether or not he had the strength to swim to it but knew he wouldn't last another night where he was. He set off, his damaged hand useless as a hand but somewhat useful as a paddle. His injury made for slow going, as the waves came toward him, pushing him back, and the wind blew in his face. He swam for what seemed like an eternity.

At last he touched the package. It was a two-man raft. It was upside down. He finally caught a wave that flipped the raft over, but he was too tired to climb in, so he simply hung on for an hour, resting. He was alone. He saw airplanes circling overhead. He gave it one more try, found the strength, pulled himself up over the edge onto the raft and collapsed.

By Thursday evening, Giles McCoy and Bob Brundige were barely conscious, awake but unaware that for the better part of the afternoon, airplanes had been circling and dropping survival gear. They'd drifted almost ninety miles since the sinking. When Giles McCoy saw the lights of the *Doyle* shining in the night, he tried to wake the others up, thinking it would give them hope if they could see the light.

The wait to be picked up was unbearable. The joy they'd felt at seeing the light in the sky didn't last. At times they were certain they'd been missed, that all the rescue aircraft and ships were already departing the scene. Night gave way to dawn, and then the sun rose directly overhead to scorch them again, and nobody came. The sun slid west, promising another night, and nobody came. Surely they would not survive another night. At four o'clock in the afternoon on Friday, a PBY flew overhead. McCoy saw men wave to them from the aircraft. Within the hour, the USS *Ringness* sailed to within fifty feet of them and sent swimmers to pull the raft alongside. McCoy said repeatedly, "I can't believe you found us," but his tongue was so swollen that his words were barely intelligible. McCoy and Brundige tried to climb unassisted the ladder the *Ringness* had hung over the side, but they were too weak. When

McCoy reached the deck, he tried to walk but fell flat on his face. Reluctantly, he accepted the offer of a stretcher, though it embarrassed him. He'd been right about one thing—the *Ringness* had indeed been leaving the scene, sailing for Peleliu, when it diverted to pick them up. They were the last survivors to be rescued, 113 hours after the sinking.

It was on the *Ringness* that McCoy was reunited with his captain, who'd been picked up earlier that morning. McVay's group had seen airplanes circling to the south on Thursday afternoon. The sight cheered McVay up somewhat, because it meant there had to be other survivors. They waited all afternoon for the rescue planes to expand their search north. None did. They filled an ammo can they'd salvaged with life preservers and rags and then fired a flare into it to light a smudge pot, but it was too little too late, the signal smoke lost in the gloom of twilight. As night fell, hopelessness returned. They saw more planes at dawn on Friday, but they were searching even farther south than they had the day before. A man in a raft presents a much higher profile than a man in the water, and will drift significantly farther in the wind. McVay's party was entirely in rafts—had they drifted completely out of the search area? The smudge pot had gone out. They decided to use the last flare they had to relight it, not because they hoped anybody would see the smoke but because they all wanted to use the flare to light the cigarette they'd saved. Weren't condemned men entitled to one last cigarette? They passed it around, knowing hope was lost. When the reignited smudge pot extinguished itself, they settled in to wait for the end to come, some praying silently, others aloud.

The *Ringness,* under the command of Captain William C. Meyer, picked them up around 10:30 Friday morning. No one had seen the smoke from the smudge pot, but the metal ammunition can McVay had used to light the fire in was large enough to kick back a radar signal to one of the search planes. Once aboard the *Ringness,* McVay proceeded to the bridge, where he helped Captain Meyer draft a message to CINCPAC headquarters at Guam that read: HAVE 37 SURVIVORS ABOARD INCLUDING CAPTAIN CHARLES MCVAY III. STATES BELIEVES SHIP HIT 0015, SANK 0030 ... 30 JULY. POSITION ON TRACK EXACTLY AS ROUTED PD [port director] GUAM. SPEED 17, NOT ZIGZAGGING. HIT FORWARD BY WHAT IS BELIEVED TO BE TWO TORPEDOES OR MINE FOLLOWED BY MAGAZINE EXPLOSION. McVay himself insisted the words "not zigzagging" be added, against Meyer's objections.

A number of ships stayed on the scene, but no other survivors were found. Of the 1,197 crew members aboard the *Indianapolis* when she sailed for Leyte, 317 men survived. Ninety-one bodies were recovered, bloated and decomposed, unrecognizable. About half of the bodies recovered afterward had been mutilated by sharks, but there's no way of knowing how many of them were dead before the sharks found them. After the bodies were identified, when identification was even possible, they were tied with two-inch line and sunk with weights, each committed to a sailor's grave. Everyone else either went down with the ship or disappeared into the deep.

Chapter Nine

The Guilty
August 2 to September 26, 1945

Leadership is a matter of intelligence, trustworthiness, humaneness, courage and sternness. The Way of the ancient kings was to consider humaneness foremost, while the martial arts considered intelligence foremost. This is because intelligence involves the ability to plan and to know when to change effectively. Trustworthiness means to make people sure of punishment and reward. Humaneness means love and compassion for people, being aware of their toils. Courage means to seize opportunities to make sure of victory, without vacillation. Sternness means to establish discipline in the ranks by strict punishments.

Sun Tzu, *The Art of War*

Knowing *how* the men in the water died is not the same thing as knowing *why* they died. The 317 men who were saved from exposure and shark attacks were asking, "Why me? Why did I live when my shipmates didn't?" The relatives of the other 880 men were asking the navy, "Why did this happen? Why wasn't the ship given an escort? Was the captain doing all he could have done to prevent attack? How could the ship go down so fast? Why weren't there more lifeboats? Why didn't anybody hear the SOSs? Why didn't anybody notice the ship was overdue in port? Why wasn't anybody keeping track of it? Why didn't somebody send rescue planes and ships immediately? What should the navy have done that they didn't do?"

As he worked on his history fair project, Hunter Scott had some of the same questions. He tried to put together a timeline of events. The more research he did, reading books and interviewing survivors, the more unfair it seemed. What went wrong, and why was Captain McVay the only one punished, when clearly he was only one of a large cast of players in the drama, and among the least culpable? Deconstructing the tragedy with the benefit of hindsight reveals a long series of errors and omissions, any one of which, taken alone, might not have meant that much, but in combination they contributed to the deaths of 880 men, and changed the lives of 317 more.

After the sinking, the relatives of the men lost had a long list of things they wished hadn't happened or weren't so. If the ship had had better ventilation, she wouldn't have been sailing under "Condition Yoke Modified" with all her hatches open and wouldn't have sunk so fast. If the ship hadn't been rushed into service to deliver the bomb to Tinian, her repairs still incomplete, no time for a shakedown cruise, with 250 new recruits on board and over 100 passengers getting in the way, her crew would have had more time to train and to practice abandon-ship drills, and perhaps would have loosened her lifeboats. If she'd sailed at top speed from Guam to Leyte to compensate for her lack of an escort, instead of sailing at 15.7 knots to conserve fuel and arrive in the morning, the *I-58* might never have caught her. If she'd been equipped with sonar, she could have detected the submarine's presence and taken evasive action. If only she'd been fully armored. If only she hadn't been top-heavy with radar and radio antennae.

There were plenty of things the navy did know that, had they been fully understood, might have prevented the disaster. There were, first of all, things the navy knew that they didn't tell Captain McVay before the *Indianapolis* left Guam. Admiral Spruance; Admiral Nimitz and his chief of staff, Commodore James B. Carter; and Captain Oliver Naquin (and possibly his assistant Lieutenant Johnson) at Marianas command all had access to information telling them that there were at least four Japanese submarines active in the southern Pacific within range of the Peddie route. They also knew that an American destroyer escort, the USS *Underhill,* had been sunk on Tuesday, July 24, three days before the *Indianapolis* arrived in Guam.

They knew because a unit identified as SIGINT, short for Signals Intelligence, had broken the Japanese communications code and had, for some time, been intercepting Japanese radio transmissions and fleet signals identifying ship locations and movements. The top-secret information SIGINT gathered was classified under the code word "ULTRA" (the same name the British gave to the information they received from cracking German communication codes). One SIGINT report showed that the *I-58* had left its base in Kure for general patrol on July 18. Another ULTRA briefing on July 23 reported that the *I-58* and the *I-367* were headed out to patrol the Marianas area west of Guam. The two subs were part of what the Japanese were calling the Tamon group, named after one of four Buddhist gods who were responsible for protecting Japan from her enemies.

Why, then, didn't anyone tell McVay about the sinking of the *Underhill* or the activities of the Tamon group? Wasn't the fact that there were four enemy subs actively hunting in the area he was sailing through something he needed to know? In part, he wasn't told because he wasn't of sufficient rank. On March 23, 1943, chief of naval operations Admiral Ernest J. King had issued a two-page directive instructing that the special intelligence developed from ULTRA be handled and distributed only by or to flag officers of commands afloat, meaning admirals. If Admiral Spruance had decided to sail to the Philippines on the *Indianapolis,* rather than fly, McVay might well have been given the information about the Tamon group or the *Underhill,* because Spruance was a flag officer. Even without revealing the source of the information or the reason for the warning, Commodore Carter might have made a casual remark, such as "Better be on your guard, Charlie—there are still Jap subs out there," when he met with McVay. At the time, however, Carter didn't know which route the *Indianapolis* would be taking, and he didn't know if Admiral Spruance would be on board or not. Anyway, Carter assumed McVay would be given the intelligence he needed at the standard predeparture briefing by Lieutenant Waldron, the routing officer. Spruance could have said something when he had lunch with McVay, but it wasn't an admiral's job to give intelligence briefings, and besides, he was planning the invasion of the Japanese home islands and had a lot more on his mind than backwater transits. Waldron should have told McVay, but Waldron didn't know, because when he called to ask about an escort, he wasn't told by Lieutenant Johnson, the assistant to surface operations officer Naquin, who'd received the information on Japanese sub activity from Commodore Carter.

Naquin, charged with plotting the locations and movements of all ships, friendly or otherwise, in the Marianas area of control, was by some accounts a cautious man, maybe a bit paranoid about security breaches, a hoarder of intelligence, some said. For whatever reason, he didn't pass the information on, perhaps because Waldron wasn't a fleet officer, so he was just following orders, or because Naquin didn't put much stock in the ULTRA information to begin with. There'd been a lot of false submarine sightings, a lot of bogus reports that never amounted to much. CINCPAC had issued a directive that capital ships sailing from Guam to the Philippines no longer needed escorts—one reasonable interpretation of that directive would have been that capital ships could take care of themselves from then on in those waters. Another interpretation might have been that without escorts, they'd need all the information they could get. The bottom line was that danger from Japanese subs was believed to be low within the jurisdiction of the Marianas command. Earlier in the war, a sub sighting like the one reported by the SS *Wild Hunter* on the 28th could have been enough to divert the *Indianapolis* from its route. As it was, Captain McVay sailed straight into harm's way without knowing it because the system created to give him the information he needed had broken down, somewhere between surface operations officer Oliver Naquin and routing officer Joseph Waldron.

The next mistake the navy made was sending the *Indianapolis* on the Peddie route without an escort. If the priority given to deploying escort ships in the waters closer to the Japanese main islands was correct, then ships sailing without escorts should probably have been given safer routes. As it was, the I-58 was waiting exactly where Captain Hashimoto knew he could expect Allied ship traffic, on a straight line between Guam and Leyte. It would have been possible for CINCPAC to have told Waldron to assign the *Indianapolis* an alternative course without compromising their ULTRA intelligence.

Perhaps the biggest mistake the navy made was losing the *Indianapolis* in the middle of the ocean. A ship sailing on a straight line at a known rate of speed should not have been that difficult to track, and yet an unlikely sequence of mechanical failures, human errors, innocent assumptions and shortsighted policies led to that result.

It wasn't unusual, for example, for a flagship to change course without notifying anyone, because a flagship served at the whim of the flag admiral who used it. Combatant ships, in general, sailed rather independently. The *Indianapolis* had sailed many times, and changed course many times, with Admiral Spruance on board (often on a straight line without zigzagging, even in combat zones), because Spruance needed to get where he wanted to go in a hurry. It wasn't unusual for a flagship not to show up when and where it was expected. Any of the commands charged with plotting ship traffic might have concluded, after the *Indianapolis* was overdue in port, that McVay had received orders they didn't know about and headed off in some other direction.

It was also common for them to assume that no news was good news—that if they didn't hear otherwise, nothing was wrong. To reduce radio chatter and to keep the Japanese from intercepting U.S. communications and learning Allied ship locations, Allied ships at sea didn't report in on a regular basis or send progress reports of how they were faring or when they thought they'd arrive. The consequence of such practices was that when they hadn't heard anything from the *Indianapolis* by 11:00 Tuesday, the plotters at the Marianas command and at CINCPAC simply assumed the *Indianapolis* had reached Leyte and took her off their plotting boards. That left only the three commands waiting for her at the other end of her transit to notice the *Indy* was missing—Admiral Oldendorf at Task Force 95, Admiral McCormick at Task Group 95.7 and the port director in Leyte, one Lieutenant Commander Jules Sancho. Of the three, the first two didn't notice, and the last one noticed but didn't say anything.

Why?

Recall the order the *Indianapolis* received from CINCPAC's advance headquarters on Guam on the 26th, two days before sailing to Leyte, that read:

> Upon completion unloading Tinian report to Port Director for routing to Guam where disembark Com. 5th Fleet personnel X Completion report to PD Guam for onward routing to Leyte where on arrival report CTF 95 by dispatch for duty X CTG 95.7 directed arrange 10 days training for Indianapolis in Leyte Area.

The directive ordered McVay to sail to Guam but didn't specify the date, saying only that McVay was to depart "upon completion

unloading," meaning vaguely whenever he was finished unloading whatever it was he had to unload. The nature of what he was unloading was,
of course, top-secret, because he was unloading the bomb. After that, he
was to take his passengers to Guam, but the directive didn't specify when
that would happen either. Finally, upon reaching Leyte, McVay was to
send a message saying he'd arrived to Oldendorf on the *Omaha,* then
sailing in the waters off Japan, and then McVay was supposed to report to
McCormick on the *Idaho* and join his task group for gunnery training in
the Philippines. Copies of the order were sent to McCormick and Oldendorf, to the port directors in Tinian and Guam, to Admiral Murray at
Marianas command, and to Admirals Nimitz and Spruance. However,
when the message was received aboard the *Idaho*, the person who decoded the message wrote down that the addressee was CTG-75.8, not
CTG-95.7. In any miscommunication, the fault may lie with the sender,
the receiver or the medium in between, and it's unclear why the *Idaho*'s
radio room got it wrong. Whatever the reason, McCormick's radio technician assumed he'd received, in effect, a wrong number, a message that
wasn't meant for him. It was only classified "Restricted," not "Top-
Secret," so he assumed it wasn't that important, and didn't ask the
sender to repeat the message. It wasn't his problem—it was CTG-75.8's
problem, whoever they were, or else it was the sender's problem.

Then at 10:40 A.M. Saturday morning, July 28, Guam routing
officer Waldron transmitted a second message containing the *Indianapolis*'s essential transit information, when it was leaving, when it
would arrive, how fast it was traveling and when it would cross "the
Chop" into the Philippine Sea Frontier. Copies of the second message
were sent to Commodore Carter at CINCPAC (who might still have
warned Captain McVay about Japanese sub activity, now that he knew
when and where the *Indy* was sailing), to Lieutenant Commander Sancho in Leyte, and to Admirals Nimitz, Spruance, Murray, McCormick
and Oldendorf. This time, McCormick decoded the dispatch correctly

and learned that the *Indianapolis* was on its way, but because he'd missed the first message, he had no idea why the *Indy* was joining his task group. He could only wait to see what was going on when she reported in, and again, because she was Spruance's flagship, chances were good that she'd divert and go somewhere else.

As for Oldendorf, he never got the second message. Waldron's communication went through the communications center in Okinawa, but there, for whatever reason, it disappeared. That meant that Admiral Oldendorf knew *why* the *Indianapolis* was coming, because he'd received the first message, but not *when*. For all he knew, she was still unloading cargo at Tinian. In other words, neither McCormick nor Oldendorf knew what was going on, and neither was directly to blame, but neither had cause to be alarmed when the *Indianapolis* didn't show up.

That left it up to the PSF or Philippine Sea Frontier, an administrative command overseeing a vast area ranging from "the Chop" at 130 degrees east longitude all the way west to Thailand, north to the twentieth parallel and south to the Dutch West Indies. The PSF oversaw local naval defenses, routing, dispatching, transport, salvage, repair, harbor control and routine shipping but had little to do with combatant ships, which were under the control of Admiral Thomas C. Kinkaid, commander of the U.S. Seventh Fleet as well as all Allied naval forces in the southwest Pacific area. At the time of the sinking, the PSF, headquartered at Tolosa on the southern part of Leyte Gulf, was run by a Commodore Norman C. "Shorty" Gillette, who had taken over only a few days earlier for Vice Admiral James Kauffman, who was away on leave. Gillette's chief of staff was a Captain Alfred N. Granum. Leyte Gulf operations were administered by NOB (Naval Operating Base) Leyte Gulf, led by Commodore Jacob H. Jacobson, with headquarters in the town of Tacloban, a city of 50,000 people midway up the gulf. The new port director in Tacloban, Lieutenant Commander Jules Sancho, 42, with the assistance of his operations officer, Lieutenant

Stuart B. Gibson, 35, watched over the arrivals and departures of over 1,500 noncombatant ships a month, about 50 a day, seeing to their berthing, servicing and provisioning. Both Sancho and Gibson were experienced naval men. It was Gibson who received the dispatch from Waldron telling him that the *Indianapolis* would arrive on the 31st. Gibson noted the information in his logbook, and mentioned it to Sancho, who mentioned it to Jacobson, though Gibson, Sancho and Jacobson were all somewhat surprised they'd been told, because it wasn't their job to keep track of combatant ships.

Philippine Sea Frontier headquarters in Tolosa maintained plotting boards keeping track of ships and planes within its jurisdiction, but it wasn't the PSF's responsibility to check the arrival times of combatant ships, or to send messages inquiring why a combatant ship hadn't arrived. Indeed, a letter from CINCPAC labeled Pacific Fleet Confidential Letter 10-CL-45 specifically ordered them not to, stating, "Arrival reports shall not be made for combatant ships." As far as the PSF and Captain Granum were concerned, the *Indianapolis* was a Fifth Fleet combatant ship, reporting to Admiral McCormick, part of a Fifth Fleet combatant ship task group, and therefore none of their business, so when 11:00 Tuesday morning came around, PSF assumed the *Indianapolis* had arrived and took her off their plotting boards. In the port director's office at Tacloban, Gibson noticed the *Indianapolis* hadn't arrived but figured if he wasn't supposed to report arrivals, then he certainly wasn't supposed to report a nonarrival, not even to his new boss Sancho (on whom he wanted to make a good impression), or Jacobson, or Granum down bay at Tolosa.

There was other information the navy failed to act on. The night of the sinking, Captain Hashimoto had radioed back to Tokyo on a standard frequency the following message: RELEASED SIX TORPEDOES AND SCORED THREE AT BATTLESHIP OF IDAHO CLASS—DEFINITELY SANK HER. Hashimoto's message was immediately intercepted, decoded and passed on by combat intelligence at CINCPAC on Guam, but intelligence assumed Hashimoto was only boasting to make himself look better to his superiors back in Tokyo. After all, there'd been no SOSs received to corroborate the claim. The message was disregarded.

Even the army contributed to the chain of errors. At four in the morning on Tuesday, July 31, the pilot of an army air force C-54, traveling from Manila to Guam, flew over the site of the sinking. Those below with working flare guns fired them at the sight of the plane. The pilot reported seeing star shells, tracers and what looked like gunfire down below, approximately 430 miles east of Manila, but the army concluded it was probably some naval action, maybe a battle between surface ships, and not the army's concern.

On August 13, to help answer everybody's questions and to determine what exactly happened, Admiral Nimitz convened a court of inquiry on Guam to investigate the sinking, even though some of the men were still lying in the hospital in the Philippines or on Peleliu recovering. The judges at the court of inquiry were Vice Admiral Charles A. Lockwood, Jr., Rear Admiral Francis E. M. Whiting and Vice Admiral Murray, Commander Marianas. The judge advocate prosecuting the case was a Captain William Hilbert. Men were questioned as soon as they could walk, but there was an odd air of secrecy about it. Nurses and corpsmen were told not to discuss the events on the ward, and survivors were warned to keep a lid on what had happened to them, lest the navy look bad in the eyes of the public. The press corps was placed under a news blackout about the sinking until the end of the war, but that wasn't unusual. One by one, the survivors were interviewed, asked to remember what had happened the night of the sinking. What was the weather like? How good was the visibility? When did they hear the order to abandon ship?

The court of inquiry interviewed forty-three witnesses, including McVay, Redmayne, Blum, Horner, Twible and fifteen enlisted men.

The court interviewed McCormick, who said it wasn't his fault because he never got the message that the *Indianapolis* was coming to train under him. They interviewed Gillette, Granum, Sancho and Gibson from PSF, but PSF blamed CINCPAC for not telling them what to do about nonarrivals (though Sancho added that Gibson never told him the *Indy* was overdue). They interviewed Carter from CINCPAC, who blamed PSF and said it was only common sense that overdue ships should be reported. They interviewed Naquin and Waldron from Marianas command, and Naquin admitted he'd known of the Tamon group but nevertheless considered the threat from submarines "negligible." The interrogation of Naquin and Waldron was compromised, some later felt, because one of the three judges ruling on the evidence was Admiral Murray, the head of the Marianas command and Captain Naquin's superior officer. Murray was, therefore, sitting in judgment of himself because it was his command's possible negligence that was being called into question. On any civilian court, a judge would recuse himself for conflict of interest.

Captain McVay attended the hearings, wondering to what extent the navy was going to blame him. He'd been made an "interested party" to the court of inquiry, meaning he'd been allowed to sit in and observe as the facts were brought out, which implied that he might be a concerned party later if the court of inquiry led to an actual court-martial. He'd given a press conference on Peleliu on August 5 and told members of the press corps the navy had, in his opinion, in so many words, messed up by failing to notice the *Indianapolis* overdue and thereby delaying rescue, so he was glad to see that officers from PSF, Marianas command and CINCPAC were being included in the questioning, but he wasn't encouraged by the way he'd been personally treated. For example, the court of inquiry issued a finding of facts on August 13, the day Captain Hilbert began his questioning, stating that his investigators had turned up a negative check of all stations that might have received an SOS. In a foreword to the court of inquiry report written the same day, Admiral Nimitz blamed McVay for failing to transmit an SOS message immediately after the explosions. Seconding that opinion, Admiral King wrote

> Measures had not been taken in advance to provide for the sending of a distress signal in an emergency. The failure of the Commanding Officer of the *Indianapolis* to have anticipated an emergency which would require the sending of a distress message on extremely short notice and his failure to have a procedure for dispatching such a message established on board ship undoubtedly contributed to the apparent fact that no message was sent. The responsibility for this deficiency must rest with Captain McVay. It is possible that mechanical failure might have precluded the sending of a distress message even if one had been available in proper form, but the record indicates no such message was ready and that this emergency had not been anticipated.

Yet McVay had ordered an SOS sent as soon as he was sure the ship was lost. Both Nimitz and King wrote their opinions believing the court of inquiry had thoroughly and accurately checked all stations that might have received an SOS, and that the people interviewed had told the truth. Both failed to take into account the possibility that if somebody had indeed received an SOS from the *Indianapolis* the night of the sinking and ignored it, with men dying as a consequence, the odds of anybody stepping forward and confessing to such negligence were indeed small.

It was going to be easier, McVay knew, to blame him for failing to anticipate the emergency than it would be to conduct a more thorough investigation. It would be easier to simply lay the responsibility on McVay's shoulders, since captains bear the ultimate responsibility for what happens to their ships.

McVay even confided his misgivings to Gil McCoy, who'd recovered fairly quickly and was serving on Guam as Captain McVay's driver. "I think they're going to hang this on me," McVay said. "How could they do that?" McCoy asked. "They have a way," the captain replied. When the court of inquiry concluded on August 20, it recommended to Admiral Nimitz that Lieutenant Gibson and Lieutenant Commander Sancho should be sent letters of reprimand for not reporting the *Indianapolis* overdue. The court also ordered Admiral McCormick to discipline his staff for failing to decode CINCPAC's July 26 cable. In McVay's opinion, Gibson was being made a scapegoat, as were McCormick's staff, and that didn't bode well. Then Judge Advocate Hilbert listed what he construed as the facts of the case regarding McVay. He maintained that Waldron had indeed warned McVay of the submarine menace, that visibility was good enough the night of the sinking that McVay should have been zigzagging, and that he'd delayed sending an SOS. The court of inquiry ruled that as a consequence, Captain McVay should be issued a letter of reprimand and court-martialed for endangering the lives of his men through negligence.

While all this was going on, the war ended in the Pacific, just over three months after it had ended in Europe on May 8. On August 6, by order of President Harry S. Truman, the *Enola Gay* dropped the "Little Boy" atomic bomb on Hiroshima, killing or injuring 130,000 people and leaving another 177,000 people homeless after destroying or damaging 92 percent of the city's buildings. On August 9, a bomb dubbed "Fat Man" was dropped on the Japanese city of Nagasaki, killing or injuring 66,000 people. The Japanese surrendered on Wednesday, August 15, finally convinced that further resistance was futile. President Truman broke the news to reporters at a press conference at seven o'clock that evening. Truman's news was monumental, given the staggering costs of the war. Three quarters of the globe's population had taken part, 1,700,000,000 people in 61 countries. One hundred ten million men and women had been pressed into military service. Twenty-five million military personnel and 30,000,000 civilians died. Six million Jews perished in the Holocaust. The United States lost over 400,000 men. Japan incurred 1,700,000 military and 380,000 civilian fatalities.

One hour after Truman's press conference, the navy issued communiqué number 622, stating, "The USS *Indianapolis* has been lost in the Philippine Sea as the result of enemy action. The next of kin of casualties have been notified." They could hardly have picked a time when the sinking was less likely to garner attention, waiting to release the news two weeks after they'd known the initial details. Newspapers carried the story of the *Indianapolis,* but the headlines screamed JAPAN SURRENDERS in hundred-point type, and right then, people didn't want to hear about another ship lost, even if it was the worst disaster at sea in U.S. naval history.

The crew of the *Indianapolis* just wanted to go home. The survivors gathered on Guam and sailed for the States in early September aboard the aircraft carrier USS *Hollandia,* riding to the pier in five buses. Gil McCoy was anxious to see his mother. She'd had a premonition the night of the sinking, waking up in the middle of the night, saying, "Gil's been hurt." A week and a half after the sinking, while her son was already recovering on Guam, a telegram had arrived at her house informing her that her son's ship had sunk and that he was missing and presumed dead, but she knew it wasn't true. He'd finally managed to get a telegram to her telling her he was okay, but he wanted to see her in person, to apologize and put his arms around her and hug her again. First he had to return the jeep he was driving to the motor pool, but when he

got there, there was a long column of trucks. He waited in line ten minutes, then twenty, then thirty, but the line was barely moving. He flagged
down a marine lieutenant and told him he was afraid if he didn't return
the jeep in time, he'd miss his ride home. The lieutenant moved McCoy
to the head of the line and arranged for a ride back to the pier, but when
McCoy got there, he was too late. His ship had sailed. His heart fell.

"You McCoy?" a sailor asked.

"Yeah," McCoy said.

"Your captain told us to wait for you," the sailor said, indicating
a small motorboat moored nearby. "Climb aboard and we'll catch that
ship for you."

They caught the *Hollandia* on the fly. McCoy jumped from the
motorboat to the ramp, elated to be able to ride home with his shipmates.
He thanked the sailors who'd ferried him out. As he climbed the ramp,
he looked up to see Captain McVay leaning out the door of the hangar
deck, personally checking to make sure his orderly made it. McVay
waved, then disappeared in the doorway. Not every captain would have
left his launch to make sure his driver didn't miss his ride home. Only
a good captain would have done that.

Chapter Ten

The Court-Martial
September 26, 1945, to February 23, 1946

All commanding officers . . . in the naval service are required . . . to take all necessary and proper measures, under the laws, regulations and customs on naval service, to promote and safeguard . . . the physical well-being and the general welfare of the officers and enlisted persons under their command or charge. A captain's responsibility for his ship is absolute.

Section 5947 of Title Ten, United States Code

The *Hollandia* arrived in San Diego on September 26. The surviving crew of the *Indianapolis* was given a parade, but the crowds were small and the celebration was relatively subdued. The men were bused to Camp Elliott, outside of San Diego, where they recuperated further, and when they were ready, they were sent home. Nineteen of them had to be taken off the *Hollandia* on stretchers, this nearly two months after the sinking. McCoy, Smith, Twible, Moseley, Bell, McGuiggan, Miner, Kuryla and the rest said their good-byes to their shipmates and went their separate ways, uncertain if they'd ever see one another again. Some took longer than others to recover from their injuries. Some put what had happened out of their minds. Others couldn't, and never would.

Captain McVay went to his home in Washington, to the comfort of his wife, Louise, and to the judgment of his father the admiral, a forty-six-year navy veteran who understood how naval justice worked. The captain's fate was in the hands of three men, Admiral Nimitz, Admiral King and the secretary of the navy, James Forrestal.

The fact that the court of inquiry had recommended that McVay be court-martialed did not require the navy to follow through with a trial. One alternative would have been simply to declare the incident an accident of war, terribly unfortunate and horribly tragic, but an accident all the same. The navy had lost 436 other combatant ships during the course of the war, and none of those ships' captains had been court-martialed, even though in each case, close scrutiny might well have revealed mistakes, omissions or errors in judgment that could have been avoided. Wartime was not the time to second-guess the men fighting it. The difference was that the war was over now. That also meant the navy could no longer suppress information or keep stories out of the newspapers by arguing that exposure could damage the war effort.

Admiral Nimitz actually argued for lenience, perhaps because he'd served in the Pacific and had seen with his own eyes what the men who'd fought the war had been through and was sympathetic, or because he was insulated by distance from the politics of postwar Washington. He was also privy to the ULTRA intelligence produced by SIGINT, and perhaps knew what the court of inquiry hadn't known—that the *Indianapolis* had been essentially sailing blind. Nimitz issued an order, five days after the court of inquiry adjourned, correcting Pacific Fleet confidential letter 10-CL-45 by stating that port directors were now to report the nonarrival of ships as soon as they were officially overdue. Nimitz recognized that he'd failed to anticipate a problem. Perhaps it seemed inconsistent to him that he was supposed to court-martial a good navy man for similarly failing to anticipate a problem, especially after he'd been kept in the dark. Nimitz had compassion for McVay, who'd met with him at Pearl Harbor on his way home to plead his case.

That didn't mean he could ignore the court of inquiry entirely or let McVay get off scot-free. Other ship captains needed to know, now and in the future, that if there was anything at all they could do to enhance the safety of their ships, they needed to do it, and the bottom line was that McVay could have been zigzagging. Nimitz needed to send a message to the other officers under his command that they needed to be on their toes and never drop their guards. That was true even though the war was over, and in fact, another war with the Soviet Union loomed in the not-too-distant future, or so it was feared. Vigilance was as important as ever. Nimitz wrote two letters. The first one, for Captain McVay's file, read:

> You erred in judgment when you failed to order zigzag courses steered on the night of the loss of the ship. The facts further indicate that you did not exert every effort at your command to cause a distress message to be sent out after the explosions and prior to the sinking. You are hereby reprimanded for the negligent manner in which you performed your duty in this instance.

Though less severe punishment than a court-martial, such a letter of reprimand in McVay's permanent file would still have effectively ended his career by preventing further promotion. They couldn't prosecute McVay for violating the standing order for ships to zigzag because his routing orders, which superseded standing orders, said he could zigzag "at his discretion." Showing bad judgment wasn't as serious an offense as disobeying an order. Nimitz's second letter, written September 6, 1945, was to the Judge Advocate General of the Navy and it read:

The Commander in Chief, U.S. Pacific Fleet, does not agree with the court in its recommendation that Captain Charles B. McVay III, U.S. Navy, be brought to trial by general court-martial. . . . His failure to order a zigzag course was an error in judgment, but not of such nature as to constitute gross negligence. Therefore, a Letter of Reprimand will be addressed to Captain McVay in lieu of a general court-martial.

Admiral King and Secretary Forrestal in Washington had other agendas. The secretary of the navy's job was to administer the nonoperational side of naval concerns. He was responsible for such things as the control of shipyards, munitions factories, bases, training, storage facilities and so on. He was also the conduit between the chief of naval operations and the President, reporting as well to Congress when there were budget or policy issues. The tragedy of the *Indianapolis* presented Forrestal with a serious public relations problem, a major disaster involving, as the court of inquiry had indicated, errors and malpractices at virtually every level of the navy. The newspapers covering the story were insisting on an explanation, asking why so many men had perished, why it had taken so long for rescue to arrive. Forrestal's office fielded bags of letters from bereaved parents wanting to know why their boys had had to die. The grieving next of kin wrote to their representatives in Congress as well, and the secretary of the navy answered to Congress. Moreover, Forrestal needed to have members of Congress on his side when he went to petition for funds or favors. There'd been talk in Congress that after the war, the navy would be unified with the army and the air force in a way that might, Forrestal feared, cost the navy its autonomy, if not its very existence. Now that the world had seen what an atom bomb could do, it looked to many, including congressional Armed

Forces Committee members, as if wars in the future would be won by air power alone. There would no longer be any need for amphibious landings or coastal bombardments, and the navy would become an anachronism, a footnote to history.

If the navy's future was in doubt, its recent past was in question as well. Immediately following the Japanese raid on Pearl Harbor, President Roosevelt appointed a commission to investigate what had gone wrong. The commission concluded that Hawaii's naval and army commanders Rear Admiral Husband E. Kimmel and Major General Walter C. Short were guilty of dereliction of duty and errors of judgment. Both men stepped down, and Congress promised a full, public bipartisan investigation as soon as the war was over. That investigation was scheduled to begin in November. The navy had done many brave and noble things during the war, and Forrestal didn't want it to be remembered merely for the disasters of Pearl Harbor and the *Indianapolis*.

Forrestal may have been under political pressure to convene a court-martial as well. One theory has it that he was pressured directly or indirectly by a man named Thomas D'Arcy Brophy, whose son Thomas Jr. had been an ensign on the *Indianapolis,* one of the new officers who'd joined the crew at Mare Island. Ensign Brophy had been in Harlan Twible's group, one of the oil-covered officers who'd decided not to identify themselves. He'd survived to the very end and only perished when he'd tried to swim to Adrian Marks's seaplane late Thursday afternoon.

Thomas D'Arcy Brophy was a powerful enough man to have access to Washington officials all the way up to President Truman. During the war, he helped organize the USO, which sent performers like Bob Hope, Bing Crosby and Betty Grable around the world to entertain the troops. Brophy was also the chairman of the National War Fund, a charitable organization that provided money for the Red Cross. One day Brophy called on Captain McVay in his temporary office at the Navy

Department in Washington, D.C., to confront the man he blamed for the loss of his boy. McVay, who'd been confronted by more bereaved accusers than he cared to count in the last month, told Brophy he had an important engagement, then went to a cocktail party to forget about his troubles for a while. Brophy's car tailed McVay's taxi all the way to the party. This was the so-called important engagement? A *cocktail party* was more important than talking to him about his boy? According to some accounts, Brophy vowed to destroy McVay, taking his demand for a court-martial to Secretary Forrestal and to the President himself.

Arguing against the theory that Thomas Brophy somehow brought about the court-martial of Captain McVay is the well-documented fact that Admiral Ernest J. King was probably the last man on earth who would ever let a civilian tell him how to run his navy. King did, however, have reasons of his own to want the court-martial. He was fiercely loyal to the navy, and would not have taken kindly to Captain McVay's August 5 press conference on Peleliu, where McVay blamed the navy for not warning him about submarine activity and for delaying rescue.

King had been the most powerful naval commander in history, with over 8,000 ships, 24,000 aircraft, 3,000,000 officers and sailors and 500,000 marines under his control. Much of the credit for how spectacularly well the navy performed during the war goes to King. He was also tactless, imperious, arrogant and difficult, with a fiery, violent temper, lecherous, a man who mercilessly hounded subordinates who made mistakes or showed weakness and an egomaniac who never admitted he was wrong. He worked his staff fourteen hours a day, seven days a week, a strenuous schedule that led one man to have a heart attack and another to commit suicide. Rather than increase his staff or reduce their hours, King merely assigned a full-time doctor to keep everyone healthy. Where Nimitz balked at the idea of dragging McVay through a humiliating public trial and thought a private letter of reprimand was all that was needed, King would have had no such compunctions. King believed firmly in punishment and in accountability, to the extent that he didn't mind occasionally punishing the innocent because it kept everybody else on their toes.

The bottom line was that King had some of the same concerns Forrestal had about protecting the navy's reputation and seeing that credit was given where it was due, and as chief of naval operations perhaps took it even more personally. After watching Congress investigate and rule on Pearl Harbor, King may have wanted to demonstrate that the navy could still take care of its own problems promptly and firmly, without anybody's help. With a massive naval force demobilizing in peacetime, he needed to demonstrate to those who remained in the navy that they would still be held responsible for their actions. King wrote a letter of his own to Secretary Forrestal on September 25 in response to Nimitz's September 6 letter, stating:

> I cannot agree with the opinion of the Commander-in-Chief, U.S. Pacific Fleet, that the failure of Captain McVay to order a zigzag course was an error in judgment . . . I recommend that the Secretary of the Navy direct the following action: Captain Charles B. McVay be brought to trial by general court-martial in accordance with recommendation 1.A of Court of Inquiry in this case.

King then ordered the navy's inspector general, Admiral Charles P. Snyder, to conduct a complete investigation into the case. Forrestal had some misgivings about the court-martial having the appearance of a show trial with the intention of making McVay into a scapegoat, and asked King to wait until Snyder's investigation was complete. King agreed on November 10, but then immediately asked Snyder if it would be feasible to court-martial McVay before the investigation was complete. Snyder said it would be. On November 12, King gave the order to proceed. It's hard to imagine a civilian court where a trial would begin before the investigation into the crime was completed, but under the code of military justice in use at the time, the navy had considerable latitude as to how it could police itself.

The charges were: 1. "Through negligence suffering a vessel of the Navy to be hazarded . . . by failing to cause a zigzag course to be steered . . . during good visibility," and 2. "Culpable inefficiency in the performance of duty . . . by failing to issue timely orders to abandon ship." Limiting the scope of the charges to McVay's actions before the sinking effectively prevented McVay's defense from raising any questions about the delay in rescue or the failure by the various commands to keep track of the ship. That, in turn, enhanced the impression that McVay and only McVay was responsible for the loss of his crew.

The trial began at 10 A.M. on Tuesday, December 4, 1945, in Building 57, a square three-story brick building painted battleship gray at the Washington Naval Yard, where McVay's father had once been in command. The weather was cold, the sky overcast. Carpenters, electricians and other craftsmen had constructed seating for over 200 spectators and a special section for the press, even though court-martials were rarely open to the public. McVay wore his best dress blues, his shoes shined to a high mirrored finish. The seven-man court facing him consisted of four captains and two commodores and was headed by Rear Admiral Wilder DuPuy Baker, a former cruiser captain and an expert on escorts and antisubmarine warfare. The judge advocate or prosecutor was a lawyer and destroyer squadron commander named Captain Thomas J. Ryan, a forty-four-year-old friend and former classmate of McVay's who'd won the Medal of Honor, two Navy Crosses and the Legion of Merit, decorations that lent considerable gravity to the arguments he made. McVay's defense lawyer was a man named Captain

John P. Cady, who'd been called in four days before the trial began, as had Ryan.

Ryan's first witness was Lieutenant Waldron, who went over the routing instructions and intelligence reports he'd given both Captain McVay and Lieutenant Janney before the *Indianapolis* sailed for Leyte. The second witness was a destroyer captain who said he would have been zigzagging, given the same intelligence reports, though of course he had the benefit of knowing that the *Indianapolis* had been sunk. The third prosecution witness was a naval astronomer who testified that the moon, on the night of the sinking, at the time of the sinking, would have been twenty-three degrees above the horizon, two days prior to last quarter, giving off an illumination equal to one quarter of a full moon, assuming the sky was clear. The fourth witness presented a report McVay had sent to Forrestal on the incident that stated there'd been "intermittent moonlight with unlimited visibility," forcing McVay to clarify that he'd been talking in the report about the moonlight while he was in the water after the sinking, not the moonlight or visibility while he was on the bridge. The fifth witness was Charles McKissick, who'd been steering the ship when McVay gave him the order to cease zigzagging. McKissick said no one was too worried about submarines, that if visibility had been good, he would have resumed zigzagging, and that he hadn't heard any order to abandon ship, though he wouldn't have been able to because he'd been far from the bridge when the explosions occurred.

Lieutenant Redmayne testified next, stating that nobody on the bridge thought it was necessary to awaken McVay once the moon began to appear intermittently between the clouds, some time after eleven o'clock, nor was anybody concerned about the submarine reports mentioned by Commander Janney. The ship's doctor, Lieutenant Commander Lewis Haynes, testified that men had joked about submarine activity at dinner. Haynes began to comment on the deaths of men in the water, only to be told by the court that it didn't want to hear about deaths in the water, and that it was in their purview only to examine evidence of negligence or inefficiency prior to the sinking.

When Gil McCoy took the stand, Ryan asked if he'd noticed the weather or the visibility once he got topside.

"Yes, sir," McCoy replied. "When I was going over the side . . . I guess the clouds just cleared the moon, and it was bright." Then on cross-examination, Cady asked him if he'd heard the word passed through the brig compartment, "All hands topside," or words to that effect. McCoy said he hadn't. He remembered the moment, the chief shouting down that they were dogging the hatch. He remembered dropping his lantern, scrambling for safety.

"Were any other people in the compartment with you?" Cady asked.

"Yes, sir. There were people sleeping down there."

"Did you notice whether they were still there when you left?"

"Yes, sir. They were starting up the ladder, sir." It was McCoy's hardest memory, one he wanted to forget but knew he never could.

The bugler, Donald Mack, testified that he'd stood on the bridge with his horn immediately after the torpedoes hit, but that nobody asked him to blow the bugle call for "Abandon ship." Ryan didn't ask Mack if he'd heard McVay tell Lieutenant Orr or Commander Flynn to pass the word to abandon ship. An Ensign Woolston, who'd only spent two weeks on the *Indy,* testified as to what caused the ship to sink once the torpedoes hit, and how many of the doors and hatches were left open to assist in ventilating the ship. Radioman First Class Joe Moran told the court about the chaos in Radio I, how they'd tried to transmit an SOS with equipment crashing all around them. The *Indianapolis*'s supply officer, a Lieutenant Reid, described how the men had all gathered on the fantail as the ship went down, and said that communications were out aboard ship. Coxswain Keyes told the court how Captain McVay had ordered him to spread the word to abandon ship, key testimony refuting the second charge. Five crew members gave accounts as to where they'd been and what they'd seen in the chaos after the first explosions—men scrambling topside, jumping into the water, officers, too. Radioman Sturtevant described what had happened in Radio I. Gunner Horner told his story. The last witness on the first day was Ensign Blum, who'd managed to get only a few hundred yards in his attempt to paddle a raft to Yap. Blum was asked, "Did anything unusual occur during the night of 29–30 July? If so, state what it was."

"The ship sank," Blum answered.

Captain Ryan resumed his prosecution the following Tuesday morning, calling the *Indy*'s former chief engineer, Commander Glen F. De-Grave. DeGrave vouched for the competency of the officers who'd been on the bridge at the time of the sinking, including Commander Lipski, Lieutenant Commander Moore and Lieutenant Orr, none of whom thought conditions had changed enough to require the resumption of zigzagging or the waking of the captain. Again, a prosecution witness's testimony supported the defense. Quartermaster Allard, who'd been keeping the weather logs, testified to the conditions that night, how there were altostratus, cirrus and cirrostratus clouds beginning at about 4,000 or 5,000 feet, the sky about six-tenths covered but clearing to the east where the moon, twenty-three degrees above the horizon, would have silhouetted the *Indianapolis* perfectly for any submarine waiting up ahead. Allard said in a closing statement that under the conditions he'd witnessed, there'd been no reason to zigzag, and that of the five captains he'd served under during his three and a half years on the *Indianapolis*, Captain McVay had been the most safety-conscious. It was clear that judge advocate Captain Ryan was trying to establish not that the *Indy* had failed to zigzag—Captain McVay had admitted as much in his initial report—but that she should have, and in that regard, he wasn't having much luck. Some seamen recalled seeing the moon, but most said it was very dark that night.

From where he was seated in the witness pool, Gil McCoy wondered how much of the helpful testimony Ryan was getting had been coerced in some way or other. McCoy wondered because he'd been called into Ryan's office shortly after being summoned to Washington and handed a statement, already typed up and waiting for him to sign. The statement had McCoy swearing that Captain McVay had failed to give the order to abandon ship. McCoy informed Ryan that he'd been nowhere near the captain when the ship went down.

"Plus there were so many explosions I couldn't have heard him if he'd been shouting into my ear."

"Nevertheless you will sign it," Ryan said. "I'm a navy captain and you're a marine private and you will do as you're told."

"Well, then, you have a whole 'nother court-martial on your hands," McCoy said defiantly, "because I'm not going to sign it. Do what you want with me."

"Get out," Ryan replied. "I'll see you later when you take the oath."

McCoy found out again on Thursday how underhanded the navy could be when he took his seat in the witness pool. He was surprised to see the person sitting next to him, a short Japanese man in his thirties who, McCoy was told, had been the captain of the Japanese submarine that had sunk them. Hashimoto was his name. As soon as McCoy learned who it was, he was outraged. What was he doing there? McCoy and the others wanted to know. No one had told them he'd be there. It was like bringing in a bank robber to testify against the guard who failed to stop the robbery. Was the navy really trying to figure out who was responsible for the deaths of almost 900 men on the *Indianapolis*? Well, here he was, sitting right in front of them in the witness booth, but instead, they were going after the captain.

McCoy wasn't the only one who was outraged. The press

covering the trial universally condemned the decision to put the Japanese submarine captain on the stand, after he'd been sent for by Admiral King's office. Countless letters to the editor agreed. Members of Congress vowed to expunge Hashimoto's testimony from the records. America was by now aware of atrocities committed by Japanese soldiers and prison commandants during the war, the "Death March" on Bataan for the survivors of Corregidor, the horrors of Santo Tomas prison in the Philippines, the starvation and beheading of American soldiers in other Japanese prison camps.

Hashimoto was asked a total of seventy-eight questions over a fifty-minute period. He was asked if he knew the difference between truth and falsehood. He was asked what his religion taught him would happen if he told a lie. Did he know what perjury was? Was he a war criminal? When the court was satisfied that Hashimoto could serve as a credible witness, the captain of the I-58 was asked about the circumstances leading to the attack, from the time he left Kure to the time he arrived at latitude 12 degrees north and longitude 135 degrees east. He drew a chart sketching the maneuvers he made as he positioned himself for the attack, and stated that the ship had been hard to see at first. By his diagram and by his description, it should have been clear to the court what a fluke it was that he'd been in that exact place at that exact time, a ship sailing straight toward him, backlit by a newly risen quarter moon directly behind her. Hashimoto said he couldn't tell if the *Indianapolis* was zigzagging or not.

"Was it zigzagging later?" Ryan asked.

"There is no question of the fact that it made no radical changes in course. It is faintly possible that there was a minor change in course between the time of the sighting and the time of the attack," the translator said. Hashimoto spoke some English, and felt that his interpreter had mistranslated his words by adding "faintly possible" when what he'd meant to say was that he'd seen small zigzag movements. When he tried to protest to the judges, he couldn't make his point in English, and the translator declined to make it for him.

"Would it have made any difference to you if the target had been zigzagging on this attack?" Ryan asked. It was the key question in Ryan's prosecution.

"It would have involved no change in method of firing the torpedoes," the translator said, "but some changes in maneuvering." In a pretrial deposition, Hashimoto had told Ryan unequivocally that zigzagging wouldn't have made any difference. Was the translator being completely accurate, or was the new qualifying phrase all Hashimoto's? Hashimoto might have added that had his torpedoes missed, he could have fired his kaitens, which were piloted. He'd also said in his pretrial deposition that visibility was good in some directions, particularly in the direction of the *Indianapolis,* but poor in others. Oddly, neither Ryan nor Cady on cross-examination asked the Japanese sub captain about the weather. Cady began his defense on Saturday, December 15, by calling six enlisted men who told the court how they'd abandoned ship. Harlan Twible testified that he hadn't gotten the word from the bridge because he was amidships, but it didn't matter because he ordered the men on the fantail to abandon ship on his own initiative. His memory was clear about the weather as well.

"When I had gone on watch, it was quite light, but later on in the evening it got so dark that I had to request that the gun captain inform me if there was a man on the shield looking out over the sea, and when it came time for me to be relieved and my relief didn't get there, I looked downwards towards the quarterdeck and noticed shapes down there, but I couldn't tell if it was one man or two," Twible told the court.

"Did you see any moon that night on the watch?" Cady asked.

"I can't recall that I did," Twible said. "There were breaks in the clouds, because I can definitely remember seeing the moon after I got in the water, but I could say that the sky was heavily overcast."

"Were you able to see the horizon?"

"No, sir."

On Monday, Cady called Marianas command surface operations officer Oliver Naquin to the stand and asked him why the *Indianapolis* hadn't been given an escort. Ryan objected to the question as irrelevant and immaterial. The court sustained the objection. Cady then asked Naquin what the risk was from Japanese subs at the time the *Indy* sailed, and Naquin replied that it was "of a low order," clarifying for the court that the three sub sightings Waldron had mentioned to McVay and Janney in his intelligence briefing were of the dime-a-dozen variety, and hadn't been borne out by any actual sinkings. Why didn't Cady ask about the ULTRA information from SIGINT regarding the Tamon group, or the July 21 Seventh Fleet intelligence center report that warned of Japanese subs active in the central Pacific area? Cady didn't ask because Cady didn't know about ULTRA. Captain Layton of CINCPAC intelligence, mindful of Admiral King's directive that ULTRA information had to be handed directly to flag officers only, had taken steps to keep SIGINT information out of both the court of inquiry on Guam and the court-martial.

Next, Captain Granum from the Philippine Sea Frontier took the stand. Cady asked him what he knew of Japanese submarine activity in his area of control, since it was Granum's job to track all ships in the area. A more aggressive lawyer might have asked Granum something like "If it was your job to track ships in the area, why didn't you track the *Indianapolis* or notice when she was overdue in port?" Ryan would surely have objected, and his objection would surely have been sustained, but it would have gotten the point across. Cady never asked that question. His best move was calling his next witness, Captain Glynn Donaho, a submarine captain with four Navy Crosses, two Silver Stars and two

Bronze Stars decorating his chest. Donaho had sunk twenty-eight vessels during the war. Of the over 4,000 ships in World War II sunk by U.S. sub commanders, most of the targets had been zigzagging. Donaho knew firsthand how ineffective the navy efforts had been.

"Based on your experience as outlined above," Cady asked, "what is your opinion of the value of zigzagging of a target as affecting the accuracy of torpedo fire?"

"With our modern submarines," Donaho replied, "fire-control equipment, high-speed torpedoes, a well-trained fire-control party, and with torpedo spreads, I didn't find that zigzagging affected the results."

"As commanding officer of a modern submarine, if you found yourself on the base course ten thousand yards ahead of a target whose normal speed—whose speed you estimated would be about twelve knots—would the normal zigzagging of this target affect the accuracy of your attack?"

"Not with a normal zigzag plan," Donaho replied.

In his cross-examination, judge advocate Ryan did his best to shake Donaho's testimony and get him to admit that zigzagging had to have some effect, however slight. Donaho said he always expected his targets to zigzag—that it was harder when they didn't, or at least more confusing. Ryan finally got him to admit that zigzagging might work if the torpedoes had already been fired. However, all you had to do to avoid that, Donaho said, was to wait for a ship to zigzag, then fire. Donaho effectively seconded what Hashimoto had said, that zigzagging really didn't make that much difference.

McVay himself was the last defense witness. To refute the second charge, he entered into the record documents containing navy instructions advising against abandoning ships too hastily, then took the stand to refute the first. He described asking for an escort from Guam. He described the visibility on the night of the sinking as poor, and tried to explain why he'd said it was good later on in his report to Forrestal.

He said the officers who were supposed to wake him if anything changed were good men who knew their duty. When Ryan cross-examined him, McVay spoke of how he'd given the order to abandon ship, and said that the officer of the deck had resumed zigzagging while McVay slept on numerous prior occasions.

Testimony ended on December 18, a week before Christmas. The next day, the two lawyers gave their summations. Cady maintained that the charges had been disproved. Ryan summarized the evidence and defined negligence as failing to do something a reasonable man would have done, or doing something a reasonable man wouldn't. "And the negligence, in this case, as we see it, is that the accused failed in his general overall responsibility to cause a zigzag course to be steered under the conditions proved, together with the fact that he failed to incorporate in his night orders, or by issuing definite instructions to commence zigzagging if and when the moon rose. He failed to issue these instructions to the officers of the deck."

Many who'd watched the trial were sure Captain McVay would be acquitted, but in the end, Ryan's argument prevailed—no matter what anybody said about how dark it was, there was enough light for Hashimoto to see and sink the *Indianapolis,* and if that was true, then McVay should have been zigzagging. He was acquitted of the charge of failing to give the order to abandon ship, but that was no surprise—the judge advocate general of the navy, Rear Admiral O. S. Colclough, sent a memo to Forrestal on November 29, 1945, admitting that the charge wouldn't hold, since only two minutes had passed between the time the ship was hit and the time the order was given. In what amounted to a virtual confession that the court-martial would be a show trial, Colclough wrote:

> This specification is recommended, however, on the ground that its use will permit Captain McVay to clear himself of criticisms made in the press. A further ground

for its use is that it will prevent any adverse remarks suggesting the impropriety of determining the sufficiency of evidence by administrative action. Full justification for ordering a trial on Charge II springs from the fact that this case is of vital interest not only to the families of those who lost their lives but also to the public at large. It is therefore respectfully submitted that Charge II should not be omitted, despite the fact that the evidence may be held insufficient.

McVay was, however, convicted of hazarding his ship by failing to zigzag. In light of Rear Admiral Colclough's November 29 memo to Forrestal, and the fact that McVay had admitted he wasn't zigzagging from the onset, clearly the reason for the trial was not to ascertain blame or mete out punishment—both could have been accomplished in other ways. Captain Charles Butler McVay III was sentenced to lose 100 numbers in his temporary grade of captain and 100 numbers in his permanent grade of commander, a relatively light punishment. The seven members of the court even went so far as to recommend clemency to the reviewing authorities.

After the trial, Admiral Spruance wrote to the chief of naval personnel saying he thought McVay a skillful captain, and that he'd be pleased to have McVay command his flagship in future operations—words that might have been more useful volunteered from the witness stand, but a sound endorsement nevertheless. Newspapers around the country supported McVay, and said he'd been misused by the navy and was taking the fall for his superiors. For his part, McVay agreed, but he was resigned to it, telling Captain Ryan, "It's for the good of the service," after his old friend apologized when the trial was over, saying it was nothing personal.

When inspector general Admiral Snyder's investigation was finally released in January, after the court-martial was over and it was too late to do McVay any good, the fuller story emerged. The report, 616 pages long, containing the testimony of fifty witnesses, indicated that his failure to zigzag had little to do with the loss of the vessel, and that McVay wasn't responsible for the rest of the tragedy, or, in navy-speak, "the causal nexus between the failure to zigzag and the loss of the ship appears not to have a solid foundation." Snyder interviewed Naquin a few days before Naquin was to testify at McVay's trial, and Naquin told Snyder what he wasn't going to tell the court, that he'd been fully aware of the Tamon group operating in the western Pacific and that that had posed an above-average threat to shipping. In the end, the inspector general's report cast the majority of the blame for the loss of lives on the Philippine Sea Frontier for not reporting the nonarrival of the *Indianapolis,* even though Snyder agreed that reporting combatant ship nonarrivals wasn't really their job. Gibson, Gillette and Granum were all given letters of reprimand, and Lieutenant Commander Sancho received a lesser letter of admonition, all for correctly implementing a flawed system. Those who created the flaws in the system escaped the consequences.

Despite the report from the inspector general, the navy maintained that its court-martial of McVay was legal and proper, on the grounds that he'd been convicted, technically, only of "hazarding" (placing at risk) his ship, and not of causing its loss or sinking. Technically, the navy was right—section 5947 of Title Ten, United States Code, warns that "commanding officers are required to take all necessary and proper measures to safeguard the physical well-being of the officers and enlisted persons under their command or charge. . . . A captain's responsibility for his ship is absolute."

The nontechnical argument that McVay would have been court-martialed for failing to zigzag even if he hadn't lost his ship is, however, rather weak, and in fact, rather preposterous. There were 436 other combatant ships lost during the war, and none of those captains were court-martialed. There were perhaps thousands of captains who at one time or another ceased zigzagging at a time when they technically shouldn't have. McVay had done it countless times with Admiral Spruance on board, and there is no record that Spruance ever told him he wasn't in compliance with section 5947 of Title Ten, United States Code. By the same argument, when Lieutenant Commander Claytor turned the spotlights of the USS *Doyle* into the night sky, he was hazarding his ship. When Adrian Marks landed his PBY-5A, he was hazarding his aircraft. True, they'd done these things to save lives. Yet if the navy was arguing that the fact of hazarding can be regarded as discrete and separate from its effect—that is, that placing the ship at risk was grounds for a court-martial no matter what happened because of it, good or bad—then by the same technicality Claytor and Marks should have been court-martialed too. The heroism of their deeds and the lives they saved would have been, by the same logic, irrelevant.

Rather than admitting they'd made a mistake in court-martialing McVay and apologizing, Secretary of the Navy Forrestal arrived at a compromise. On February 20, 1946, Forrestal signed a statement approving the proceedings, findings and sentences of McVay's court-martial but added that in light of his service to the navy, his numerous commendations and his Silver Star and Purple Heart medals, "and further, in view of the unanimous recommendation to clemency signed by all members of the court, the sentence is remitted in its entirety. Captain McVay will be released from arrest and restored to duty."

On February 23, at a press conference at the Pentagon headed by Admiral Nimitz, who'd replaced King as chief of naval operations, the navy issued a nine-page press release entitled "Narrative of the Circumstances of the Loss of the USS *Indianapolis*," based on Snyder's investigation, written by Vice Admiral Forrest P. Sherman, but when Sherman submitted an early draft to his superiors for their comments, a paragraph describing what Naquin knew from ULTRA information produced by SIGINT was deleted. Also cut was a paragraph admitting that CINC-PAC had kept the information from McVay when he'd met with Commodore Carter on Guam. A short time later, Secretary Forrestal withdrew the letters of reprimand against Gibson, Gillette and Granum and the letter of admonition against Sancho, leaving only McVay to shoulder the blame.

The fact that McVay's sentence had been remitted mattered very little to the family members who were still grieving, still looking for someone to hold accountable. Some agreed with the newspapers and felt McVay had been unfairly treated by the navy, but others disagreed. It wasn't McVay against the navy, McVay *was* the navy, he was the navy's chief representative on the ship, and their boys were gone because of him.

Chapter Eleven

The Price
1946–1997

These are the men whose minds the Dead have ravished.
Memory fingers in their hair of murders,
Multitudinous murders they once witnessed. . . .
Therefore still their eyeballs shrink tormented
Back into their brains, because on their sense
Sunlight seems a blood-smear; night comes blood-black,
Dawn breaks open like a wound that bleeds afresh.

Wilfred Owen, "Mental Cases"

There are two basic ways to react to danger. We can either stand our ground, or we can run away. It's referred to as the fight-or-flight response, describing how the autonomous nervous system, the involuntary part of the brain that controls things like breathing and swallowing, prepares the body for conflict. When a dog gets within thirty feet of a squirrel in a park, the squirrel becomes hyperalert, freezing in place, muscles tensed, heart racing to increase energy output, and when the

139

dog closes the distance, the squirrel takes flight and runs to the nearest tree. When a cat is cornered by a dog and can't run away, the cat arches its back to appear larger than it is, extends its claws, bares its teeth, its heart pumping, its adrenaline releasing, and if the dog closes the distance, the cat fights back. Once the danger has passed and the squirrel is safely up the tree, the squirrel's nervous system resets itself to the default position. It doesn't think about it anymore. Once the cat drives the dog off, the cat doesn't retain any anger toward the dog, or wonder why the dog chose to attack it and not some other cat, and doesn't ask itself whether or not it was a good cat or a bad cat for responding the way it did—its nervous system simply resets itself to the default position, and the cat goes about its business.

The human nervous system doesn't always reset itself so quickly after a life-threatening experience. It can happen when we find ourselves in a situation of great violence or danger, where we can neither fight *nor* flee. Instead we experience an overwhelming sense of powerlessness and loss of control over our lives—imagine the squirrel locked in a small room with the dog, or a cat that's been wounded and can't lift a paw to defend itself. For humans, it can happen when we're assaulted or attacked, and it can happen in war. Such events cause not only physical injury, but psychic injury called trauma, and trauma does damage to the autonomous nervous system. Though the damage can't be X-rayed or seen with the naked eye, it's as real as a broken arm or leg.

When that psychic injury fails to heal, or evolves over time to become a permanent part of the victim's life—when the reset button doesn't work anymore—it's called post-traumatic stress disorder. In military parlance, it was called "shell shock" during World War I and "combat fatigue" during World War II.

Three hundred and seventeen men survived the sinking of the *Indianapolis,* which meant that there were 317 different stories to be told afterward. The men who came home weren't the same men who'd left.

The USS *Indianapolis* off Mare Island, California, July 10, 1945. (National Archives)

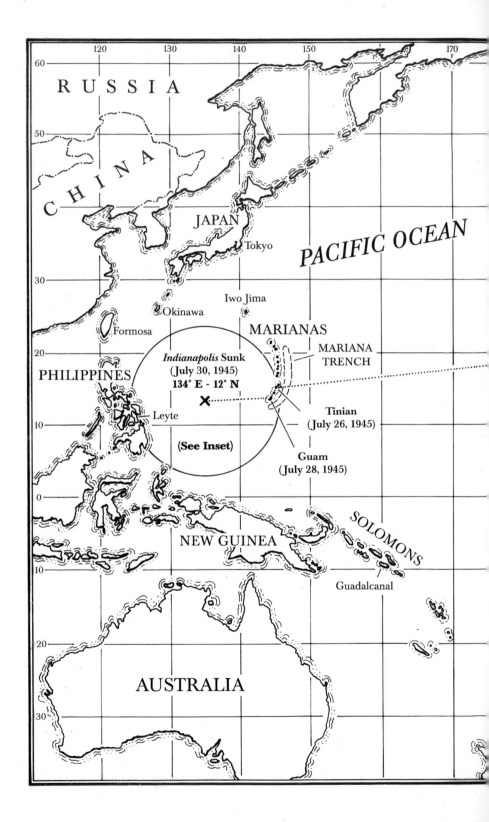

120   130   140   150   170

60

RUSSIA

50

CHINA

JAPAN

30   Tokyo   PACIFIC OCEAN

Iwo Jima

Okinawa   MARIANAS

20   Formosa   MARIANA
TRENCH

PHILIPPINES   *Indianapolis* Sunk
(July 30, 1945)
134° E - 12° N

Leyte   ✕   Tinian
(July 26, 1945)

10   Guam
(July 28, 1945)

(See Inset)

0

NEW GUINEA   SOLOMONS

10   Guadalcanal

20

AUSTRALIA

30

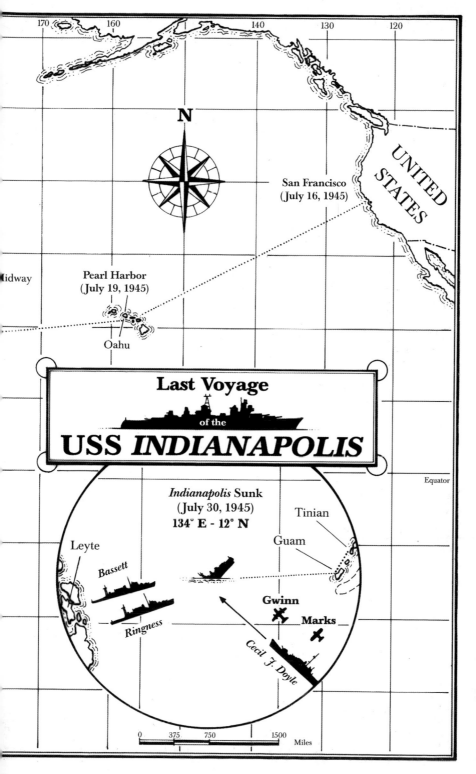

N

San Francisco
(July 16, 1945)

UNITED
STATES

Midway

Pearl Harbor
(July 19, 1945)

Oahu

Last Voyage
of the
USS *INDIANAPOLIS*

Equator

Indianapolis Sunk
(July 30, 1945)
134° E - 12° N

Tinian

Guam

Leyte

Bassett

Gwinn

Marks

Ringness

Cecil J. Doyle

0   375   750   1500

Miles

Map created by Rick Britton

170   160   140   130   120

Hunter Scott reviewing his research.

Hunter Scott speaking at a press conference in Washington, D.C. Congresswoman Julia
Carson is on the left (wearing a purple scarf) and Congressman Joe Scarborough
on the right (wearing a gray suit).

Hunter Scott with survivor Morgan Moseley.

Hunter Scott with Adrian Marks, the pilot who landed his PBY-5A in the water
and rescued many sailors.

Maurice Bell shows Hunter Scott his Purple Heart.

Congressman Scarborough and Hunter Scott with his history fair exhibit.

Hunter Scott at the USS *Indianapolis* memorial.

Hunter Scott preparing to speak to the Veterans of Underage Military Service.

Hunter Scott with some of the *Indianapolis* survivors and Senator Bob Smith (wearing a dark suit), a key figure in the effort to clear Captain McVay's name.

Some were changed greatly and permanently, some were changed only slightly and temporarily, but all 317 men experienced trauma and each man dealt with it in his own way.

The symptoms of post-traumatic stress would have varied from man to man, depending on each one's personality, the support group he returned to and the nature of his experiences in the water. Generally speaking, a sailor or soldier suffering from post-traumatic stress disorder might find himself on an emotional or psychic roller coaster, moving from times when the past intrudes suddenly on his consciousness to times when he feels almost numb to it. He can feel intense emotions without remembering what happened to him, or he can remember every detail of what happened but feel nothing. The sound of water splashing in the kitchen sink while he's reading the newspaper in the next room can become the sound of a shark's fin pushing against a wave, and without his knowing why, suddenly his heart races, his blood pressure spikes, he breaks into a sweat and the hairs on the back of his neck stand on end. Memories of being in danger spontaneously interrupt his stream of thought, so that he can have flashbacks while he's awake and nightmares when he's asleep, nightmares that can recur for years.

After a while, maybe three to six months after the traumatizing event, these intrusions begin to attenuate, lessening in frequency and intensity, but it doesn't necessarily mean he's recovering, rather that a kind of numbness is setting in. In severe cases it's called post-traumatic amnesia. The sufferer constricts his field of consciousness or willfully suppresses his thoughts, trying to close out the feelings or images that upset him. A good many PTSD sufferers intentionally numb themselves with drugs or alcohol to wash away the feelings of helplessness and terror. The quality of a sufferer's life becomes diminished by a general lack of openness or generosity, because he's playing it safe without knowing he's doing it, closing himself off to a danger that has long since passed.

The intrusions become fewer and farther between, but the net effect over time is a distortion of reality, until the sufferer can feel disconnected from the world around him, like he's just pretending to be himself, or going through life more as an observer than as a participant. Combat veterans suffering from PTSD frequently feel unresolved guilt about the things they did and, often more troubling, things they could have done differently to change the outcome.

Many of the men who came home from World War II didn't want to talk about it. They wanted to put it behind them, let it rest, forget about it, and besides—what could they possibly say that would convey the truth of it anyway?

Robert McGuiggan and Mike Kuryla both worked construction in Chicago after the war, McGuiggan as a bricklayer. He helped erect the Sears Tower. At the time it was built, it was the tallest building in the world. Radio Technician Jack Miner went to work for his father's lampshade materials company and eventually took it over. For fifty years, off and on, he has thought about his friend Ray. His nightmare was about not being able to hold Ray's head out of the water. For a long time, he wondered if anyone had ever heard the SOS he helped send.

Harlan Twible stayed in the navy until 1947, then went into the reserves and got called up again in 1951 during the Korean conflict. He served as vice president of an electrical manufacturer in Indiana and retired to Florida. For a while, he had dreams where the *Indianapolis* was sailing straight into his bedroom. He didn't speak about the sinking until 1989, in part because he didn't want his life to be defined by a single event, as catastrophic as it may have been. He didn't care to be known primarily as the survivor of a shipwreck. When he realized that for the most part kids don't really know much about World War II, their

grandfathers' war, and therefore don't appreciate that freedom is something you occasionally have to fight for and protect, he started speaking
up, and is often invited to speak at schools.

The navy wanted Morgan Moseley to reenlist and offered to promote him to chief, but he decided he'd had enough of cooking for the
navy and got out November 12, 1945, four days before his twenty-
fourth birthday. He went to work for the railroad. In June of 1949, he
married his wife, Joy, and with her raised four daughters. Moseley
bought a farm in north central Florida, where he raised and sold cows.
It's the kid he couldn't help who haunts him. He has nightmares almost
every week. He still sees the boy in the hatch, his black hair, his flushed
complexion, the apprehension on his face. One second he was right
there, almost out, and the next second he was gone. He was a good kid.
All he ever asked for was a midnight snack. He'd probably been on his
way to the galley when the ship sank. Why didn't he climb out when he
had the chance? More to the point—why, Moseley thinks, didn't he let
the kid go first? Why didn't he let him climb through the hatch first?
That's all he had to do.

Cozell Smith went to work for Sun Oil in the marketing department, helping build roadside travel marts, traveling a great deal and
moving among Oklahoma, Missouri and Tennessee. He was a happy guy
who liked to tell jokes and entertain friends, but his outer life didn't always reflect his inner life. After the war, he had recurrent nightmares
about being in the water, and would kick his legs violently in his sleep as
if swimming, until his wife had to get out of the bed and shout at him
from across the room to wake him up. She didn't dare grab him or try to
hold him still, because in his dreams, the shark was pulling him down

again, taking him by the hand and dragging him into the darkness. On several occasions while on the road on business, staying alone in a hotel, Cozell Smith made so much noise in his sleep that the people in the adjoining rooms called the police. He never talked with his family about what had happened to him, but toward the end of his life he spoke on the telephone almost daily with one of his shipmates, a man named Buck Gibson, and they agreed that in many ways, the ones who had gone down with the ship were the lucky ones. Images troubled him, particularly the image of a man slitting another man's throat to drink his blood. It got worse as he got older. In retirement, with more and more time on his hands, he began to wonder what the purpose of his surviving was. He could have died but he didn't—why? Near the end, he began seeing a psychologist at the VA hospital in Tulsa, who encouraged him to write down his thoughts and feelings. His son Michael never really knew what his father had been through until he read the essay, entitled "For Peace of Mind." Cozell Lee Smith passed away in October of 1996.

When Gil McCoy got back to St. Louis, he felt glad to be alive and determined to do something important with his life. He'd been given a second chance, he felt, and he wanted to make the most of it, though first he had a favor to do for a friend. He'd promised a hometown pal named Harry, whom he'd run into on Guam, that when he got back to St. Louis he'd look his fiancée up and maybe take her to a movie, keep her company until Harry got back. Anything for a friend. Her name was Betty Goldbeck and she turned out to be the love of Gil McCoy's life.

In 1958, McCoy was living in Boonville, Missouri, when he got a surprise visit from Felton Outland, one of the last five men on McCoy's raft. Outland had read a book on the sinking called *Abandon Ship!* by a man named Richard Newcomb, published that year, which laid out the narrative of the sinking and the injustices done to Captain

McVay. Outland felt moved to drive all the way from North Carolina to thank the man who'd saved his life. The reunion was tearful and joyous and it got McCoy to thinking—maybe it would do some of the other survivors some good to get together again and check in with one another. He even consulted with a psychiatrist at the University of Missouri and asked his advice. He was able to track down 220 of the 317 men who'd made it out of the water. The reunion was held in July of 1960 at a hotel in downtown Indianapolis, the city the ship had been named after.

McCoy knew they needed to talk. A closed-door session was set up, no wives allowed, with a sergeant at arms at the door to make everyone feel secure that they wouldn't be overheard or interrupted.

Men arranged themselves as best they could according to the groups they'd been with in the water fifteen years before, and then they testified, confessed—got things off their chests that they'd been carrying with them for years, things they'd done and things they'd seen. They talked about their nightmares. Some didn't speak but only nodded, thinking, *Yeah, I did that. I felt that. I remember that.* Men cleansed themselves, atoned, apologized, said their piece and bawled like babies. For some, it was too hard, too intense. The session didn't last more than a few hours. The survivors came away from it with an understanding that every man has a breaking point and it's nobody's fault when he breaks.

McCoy had hoped the bad dreams would stop entirely after the reunion, but they didn't. They became more integrated into his life, and he didn't feel quite so alone, knowing he wasn't the only one having them, and that if he wanted to, there were other survivors he could talk to. In his dreams, he still heard the screams of the men who'd been trapped below after he'd climbed through the hatch. He still saw the glint of the battle lantern he'd left behind shining through the crack just before the hatch was dogged. What if there was just one more guy he could have freed? What if the men who went down with the ship blamed

145

him, or cursed his name as the compartment filled with water to drown them all? By the light of dawn, he didn't blame himself and knew he'd done everything he could, but at night, in his dreams, he still heard their voices and saw their faces and wondered why he'd lived and they hadn't, why he'd been lucky and they hadn't, or if it wasn't luck, why God had spared him and not them.

What the survivors accomplished at their first reunion, and what they continued to do at subsequent reunions, was to begin the healing process by establishing a way to put the story into words, enabling those survivors who needed to, to speak about things that felt unspeakable. The reunion gave Gil McCoy and everyone else who'd attended a renewed sense of community and, more importantly, a renewed sense of purpose. To a man, the survivors came away from the reunion with the conviction that their captain had been unfairly court-martialed, hung out to dry and used as a scapegoat by the same navy that had left them in the sea to die. This was the part of their collective story that was still out of balance, the wrong that needed to be righted.

They'd invited Captain McVay to the first reunion and met him at the airport, standing at attention and saluting him as he stepped down from the plane with his wife, Louise. He broke down and cried. His father had died the year before—if only he could have seen this reception. Captain McVay had been hesitant to come, certain that some of his men still hated him for what had happened to them. He found the opposite was true. They embraced him and told him they didn't blame him. Gil McCoy suggested over drinks in his hotel room late one night with McVay that the captain had gotten a raw deal, and that perhaps there was something to be done to clear the captain's name. McVay demurred, saying (despite the endorsements of his crew) that he'd gotten what he deserved.

How did he come to feel that way?

After the court-martial, McVay took a desk job at the naval air station outside of New Orleans. Even though he'd had his sentence re-mitted, he knew he wasn't going anywhere, and that he'd never get an-other ship. After he'd put in his thirty years of military service, he retired on June 30, 1949, at the age of fifty. He was promoted to rear admiral upon retirement, but that was standard practice, a "tombstone promo-tion," it was called, one that didn't reflect or imply any sort of exonera-tion. Afterward he still preferred to be called captain, not admiral. He got a job working for an insurance company, later for an employee ben-efit consulting firm. Some of his friends found him cheerful and fun-loving, while others found him reserved and distant. Some noticed that he didn't whistle anymore, and frequently seemed lost in thought.

When his beloved Louise died of lung cancer a year after the first reunion, his heart broke. He later got remarried to a socialite named Vivian Smith, a woman he'd known since his youth and dated back in the thirties. The couple moved to her farm in Litchfield, Con-necticut, where he kept himself busy with small projects between ex-cursions into Litchfield high society. In 1965, his favorite grandson died of a brain hemorrhage at the age of nine.

Perhaps hardest of all for McVay to bear were the cards and let-ters he received from the families of the sailors who died when the *Indi-anapolis* sank, hate mail blaming him and asking him how he could live with himself, even Christmas cards from families telling him how he'd ruined their Christmases forever because he'd killed their sons. Louise had tried to screen his mail for him and keep him from seeing the hate mail, but she was never entirely successful. Since her death, he'd col-lected a large number of letters, which he saved in bundles bound by string or rubber bands.

On Wednesday, November 6, 1968, Charles Butler McVay spent the morning on his farm helping his gardener, a man named Al Dudley, prepare the shrubs and flowers for winter. A gravel drive led to a pair of barns behind the house, one converted to a four-car garage, the other a toolhouse, with an old gas pump between them. A faded hex sign deco-rated the back barn. The temperature was in the high forties, the day overcast with rain predicted that evening. The newspaper that day re-ported on the presidential election held the day before between Richard Nixon and Hubert Humphrey, but by the time the paper went to press, it was still too close to call. The back pages told of postponed peace talks in Paris to end the war in Vietnam, violent student election protests, kids carrying coffins and Viet Cong flags down Fifth Avenue in New York City to protest what the military was doing in Southeast Asia. The world had changed a great deal since 1945.

That afternoon, McVay's housekeeper, Florence Regosia, no-ticed his lunch was still untouched, so she went to his room, where she saw an empty holster on the night table. She'd just checked to see if the car was in the garage when she heard a shot. She went to the back door, where she ran into Al Dudley coming up the flagstone steps. The gar-dener had found the body in the front yard. The bullet had entered McVay's skull on the right side. His .38-caliber service revolver was in his right hand. He held his house keys in his left hand. Attached to the key chain was a small toy sailor, a gift he'd received as a boy that he'd car-ried as a good-luck charm. He died a few hours later in the hospital. Charles Butler McVay III's ashes were eventually scattered over the Gulf of Mexico, where seven years before he'd strewn the ashes of his true love, Louise.

Efforts by the survivors to clear the captain's name were already under way when they heard of the suicide. The tragedy only spurred them to redouble their efforts. They organized, looked for information, wrote letters to the navy, appealed to their senators and congressmen. As chairman of the *Indianapolis* Survivors' Association, Giles McCoy peti-tioned President Ford in 1975 to grant the survivors a Presidential Unit Citation, only to be turned down. The case was also investigated in 1975 by Senators Vance Hartke and Thomas Eagleton, without results. When

Louise McVay's cousin Graham Claytor, the captain of the USS *Doyle,* became secretary of the navy under President Carter, McCoy and the others held out hope for McVay's exoneration, only to be told there was nothing Claytor could do. McCoy petitioned President Reagan in 1980 for a Presidential Unit Citation, but he was again told the *Indianapolis* did not meet the criteria for such an award. A second plea to Reagan in 1983 was answered: "All avenues of appellate review have long been exhausted. No authority exists for the Secretary of the Navy or the Judge Advocate General to change the findings. . . ." A presidential pardon had been eliminated as an option when Secretary Forrestal remitted McVay's sentence back in 1946—a president couldn't pardon McVay because technically he'd already been pardoned.

In 1992, Republican Senator Richard Lugar of Indiana, who was born in Indianapolis, requested that an Indiana law firm do a legal study of the court-martial, but nothing changed. An account by the Department of the Navy entitled *Report on the Court-Martial of Captain Charles B. McVay III, USN, Commanding Officer, USS* Indianapolis, drafted in March of 1996 in response to three separate inquiries by representatives, again supported the findings of the court-martial.

For all their letters and all their lobbying, it looked to the survivors of the USS *Indianapolis* as though the navy was going to win. It was going to wear them down and prevail by sheer attrition, the institution outlasting a group of old sailors, many of whom were frail or sick. More were dying each year. They'd promised themselves they wouldn't stop trying to clear their captain's name, but their hopes seemed dim, their chances remote—until an eleven-year-old boy named Hunter Scott started a history fair project in Pensacola, Florida.

Chapter Twelve

The Boy's Crusade
May 1997 to October 2000

Political interest can never be separated in the long run from moral right.

Thomas Jefferson

After interviewing Maurice Bell, Hunter Scott had contacted all of the 154 survivors still alive, using a directory of names and addresses that Bell had given him. He'd sent each survivor a questionnaire, asking questions such as, "Where were you when the torpedoes hit?" and "Did you see any sharks?" Of the 154 survivors to whom he'd sent letters, 83 responded. Some men replied only briefly with curt one-sentence answers, as if it was still something they didn't want to talk about, but others sent him envelopes full of material, including multiple-page personal narratives they'd written out in longhand or typed up years before on old Smith-Corona typewriters with faded letter *M*s and ink-filled *e*s. Harlan Twible sent Hunter chapters from a book he was working on about his life. Others sent newspaper or magazine articles they'd saved over the years. Morgan Moseley gave him the telegram the navy had sent Moseley's mother, telling her her son was a

151

casualty, which she assumed meant her son was dead. Hunter had even managed to contact Mochitsura Hashimoto, now a retired Shinto priest, who'd sent him a vintage and somewhat sinister-looking auto-graphed black-and-white photograph taken of the Japanese captain as he stood at his periscope.

For his project Hunter also had a photo of Captain McVay and one taken of the *Indianapolis* just before she'd sailed from Hunters Point. He had a map of the South Pacific, with the spot marked where the *Indy* had sunk, as well as newspaper articles from 1945 and pictures taken at the court-martial. He'd printed out and mounted brief para-graphs telling the story of the sinking, the reasons why rescue had been so tragically delayed, as well as quotes from some of the survivors stat-ing what an injustice it was that their captain had been court-martialed. He had a flowchart illustrating the various military jurisdictions. He had letters from survivors, first-person accounts of how they'd suffered in the water for four and a half days, collected in a pair of three-ring notebooks. He also had notes from them wishing him luck, many ex-pressing the hope that perhaps his project would help them in their quest to clear their captain's name. After fifty years without success, it would have been hard to say how many of the survivors truly believed that Hunter's project would do much good, but Hunter believed it. As far as he was concerned, he'd been passed a torch, commissioned to right a wrong.

Hunter's project won first prize at his school and first place at the county-level competition. In the state finals at the Florida history fair competition in May of 1997, his project was disqualified when his display of three-ring notebooks proved to constitute a minor rules infraction. A girl with a rock collection did better, though Hunter was hard put to un-derstand what rocks had to do with either Triumph or Tragedy. When he failed to win he took it hard, partly because he had the sense he'd disap-pointed people who'd been counting on him. He wrote notes to over sixty of the survivors when he got home. They wrote him back, telling him they appreciated his efforts to help, and never to give up. If anybody knew about not giving up, Hunter figured, they did.

A week later, a member of his church had a suggestion. He had an office where a lot of people came and went every day, plenty of foot traffic—maybe Hunter could set up his display in the office for a while? It was better than letting it sit in storage. The office belonged to a man named Joe Scarborough, a friend of Hunter's parents as well as Florida's Republican congressman from the First District. The congressman spent the majority of his time in Washington, D.C., but kept an office in downtown Pensacola.

Two weeks later, Hunter got a phone call from a man named Steve Mraz, a reporter for the Pensacola *News Journal.* He'd gotten a call from a couple of people who'd visited Representative Scarborough's office and wanted to write a news story about Hunter's project and the effect it was having. Pensacola was, after all, a navy town—a lot of the reporter's readers would probably be interested in learning about the kid out to reverse a fifty-year-old injustice done by the navy to one of its own. The story ran on June 26, 1997, with the headline SHIP BECOMES STU-DENT'S MISSION. The piece had all the components of a classic human interest story. The next day it went out over the Associated Press wire and was picked up by newspapers across the country. One of those papers was the *Litchfield County Times.* Litchfield, Connecticut, was where Captain McVay had lived just before taking his own life. It was also the home of *NBC Nightly News* anchorman Tom Brokaw, who saw the article on Hunter and thought he'd be perfect for a series Brokaw was doing on ordinary Americans making a difference in American life.

When a producer for *NBC Nightly News* named Barbara Raab called and told Hunter they wanted to feature him on a segment they were calling "The American Spirit," Hunter began to understand exactly how he could help. The facts, he'd always believed, could speak for

153

themselves, and it was his job to help organize and present the facts, even uncover new ones. It wouldn't matter if no one was listening. He could make people take notice, simply because he was so young, and it was unusual for someone so young to be involved in such a thing. "A middle school history fair project that seeks to correct history," the papers often said.

The *NBC Nightly News* program aired its "American Spirit" segment on August 1, 1997, two days after the fifty-second anniversary of the sinking. The Indianapolis *Star* had carried a story about Hunter five days earlier when he'd attended his first USS *Indianapolis* Survivors' Organization reunion in the city of Indianapolis, accompanied by an NBC film crew. The survivors were old men, some of them in wheelchairs or walking with canes, accompanied by silver-haired wives all better-looking than their men. Hunter was welcomed by survivors he'd only corresponded with or talked to on the phone: Loel Dene Cox (seaman second class) from Comanche, Texas; Harold Eck (seaman second class) from New Orleans; and Woodie James (coxswain) from Salt Lake City, men who shook his hand and treated him like a grandson. When they saw the television cameras following him, they told him maybe he was just what they needed to get this thing done, to clear the captain's name. Few of them had any interest in looking like heroes, but they welcomed the publicity, simply because injustice is like the shadow cast by wrong—shine enough light on a shadow and it goes away. Hunter was most impressed by a meeting with Adrian Marks, then in a wheelchair, the saving angel who'd landed his Dumbo in twelve-foot seas and risked his own life to save the lives of others. He also met Charles McVay IV, the captain's son, dubbed "Quatro" because he was the fourth in his family with that name. Quatro told Hunter he was thrilled by what Hunter was trying to accomplish.

After the NBC news segment with Tom Brokaw, the phone in the Scott household wouldn't stop ringing. Reporters who wanted to know more called from newspapers all across the country. Eventually

Hunter's story would run in newspapers in eighteen countries. He received calls as well from National Public Radio's *All Things Considered* show and *ABC World News Tonight.* One phone call brought an invitation to visit Honolulu, home of Captain McVay's son Kimo, who'd been trying to exonerate his father for over fifty years and who told the press, regarding Hunter, "He's gotten farther in a few months than the survivors and I have in half a century. Now we're pinning our hopes on him."

Kimo McVay turned over all his files to Hunter, giving him letters Captain McVay had written; transcripts of his testimonies at the court of inquiry and court-martial; copies of letters Kimo had written to various congressmen over the years; the dog tags Captain McVay had worn when he was at the Naval Academy, his thumbprint etched permanently on the back; and even Captain McVay's cigarette lighter, engraved with a picture of the *Indianapolis,* which Kimo wanted Hunter to have. Hunter visited Honolulu in November of 1997, where he was given a ride on the nuclear submarine USS *Indianapolis,* namesake to the *Indy* that had sunk in 1945. After his submarine ride, Hunter felt more resolved than ever that when he grew up, he wanted to join the navy. On November 20, Honolulu Mayor Jeremy Harris proclaimed it Hunter Scott Day, and the story was carried by the Honolulu *Star-Bulletin* and the Honolulu *Advertiser.*

Every sound bite helped. Where some people seek fame for the rush of seeing their name in print, Hunter appreciated the attention that came his way more because it served two purposes. First, it helped him gather information about the *Indianapolis,* because people sent him pieces of the puzzle with letters saying, "Dear Hunter—I never knew whom to tell this to until I saw your picture in the paper." Second, it opened doors. Kimo McVay had worked as an entertainment promoter in Hawaii and knew the value of publicity. When Representative Scarborough suggested that Hunter accompany Kimo McVay and a group of survivors on a trip to Washington to lobby Congress, Hunter accepted. Kimo contacted an old acquaintance in January of 1998, an ex-lobbyist named Mike Monroney, labeled in various magazines over the years as one of the 100 most influential people in Washington, D.C. He'd followed the court-martial in the newspapers when it was happening, and had always felt outraged at the way Captain McVay was treated by the navy. Monroney told Kimo that although he was retired, he'd be happy to help, and ended up helping to draft resolutions, write letters, set up meetings and handle the press.

What Hunter and Kimo and the survivors were hoping for was some way to clear Captain McVay's name. They hoped somebody could overturn or reverse the verdict passed down by the court-martial board back in 1945, or expunge the conviction from McVay's record, or at least force somebody from the navy to admit they'd made a mistake and were sorry about it. Passing a bill in Congress is as simple as writing it up and then getting everyone in both the House and the Senate to read it and then a majority to vote in favor of it; which is to say, it's not simple at all. First, a bill needs sponsors, senators or representatives willing to go to bat for it by lending their name and their clout. It has to be written in such a way as to comply with all the preexisting rules and codes of Congress, in language that can be agreed upon by as many people as possible, both Democrat and Republican. Then, before it can be brought to the floor, it has to be discussed and voted on in all the relevant subcommittees. In the case of a congressional resolution reversing a navy court-martial, such a piece of legislation would have to be discussed in the Armed Services Committees of both the House and the Senate.

To move a bill through Congress, all the various technicalities, personal relationships and internecine power struggles have to be finessed, like a video game such as Myst or Dungeons and Dragons, where the object is to navigate through a labyrinth fraught with peril. The common denominator is that most senators and representatives, regardless of party, want to look good in the newspapers. Some care more about their image than others, but the bottom line is that to get re-elected, a congressperson needs all the good publicity he or she can get, and Hunter Scott represented a chance to do the right thing and get good publicity in the process.

There were five television cameras waiting for Hunter at the airport when he arrived in Washington in the third week in April of 1998. Mike Monroney found that where ordinarily a press agent contacts the media hoping to get some ink or airtime, in Hunter's case, the media were calling him, asking for interviews and hoping to book Hunter on all the talk shows. In four days, beginning April 21, Hunter met with numerous senators and congressional representatives. Most encouraging were his meetings with Speaker of the House Newt Gingrich, then probably the most powerful man in Congress, who pledged his support, and with Senators Daniel Inouye (Democrat of Hawaii) and Robert Smith (Republican of New Hampshire), who said they'd help on the Senate side. Hunter and the survivors were discouraged only by a meeting with Representative Steve Buyer, the chairman of the House Armed Services Committee, who sounded like he thought they were trying to rewrite history. Hunter didn't see why you shouldn't rewrite history, if what has been previously written is wrong.

At their meetings with congressmen, Hunter and the survivors essentially told their side of the story, with Hunter taking the role of spokesman, often to the amazement of those present, a twelve-year-old with a better grip on the facts than any of the grown-ups. At the end of each meeting, Hunter boldly asked each congressperson or senator if he could count on his or her support, often in front of news cameras. Hunter had practiced talking about the *Indianapolis* with his dad, fielding questions and rehearsing to make sure his answers were concise and to the point, both to help him deal with the media and to help him in his meetings in Washington. When Senator Smith asked him if his evidence was solid, Hunter didn't waver in his answer.

"As a rock, sir," he replied, shoving his research across the table to the New Hampshire senator.

The entire room burst into laughter.

On the twenty-second of May, Hunter and the others held a press conference in front of the U.S. Capitol, where Hunter fielded questions from fifteen different television news crews and dozens of newspaper, magazine and radio reporters, after which Hunter had the honor of dropping House Resolution 3710 into the hopper of the House of Representatives. He was escorted by Scarborough, a Republican, and by Representative Julia Carson, a Democrat who represents Indianapolis, Indiana. At one point the sergeant at arms who guards the door told Representative Carson that children weren't allowed on the house floor, but Carson whisked Hunter past the guard, explaining that Hunter was her son, even though Representative Carson is African American and Hunter is not. The resolution sought to erase all mention of McVay's court-martial and conviction from his military records, and to award a Presidential Unit Citation to the survivors. Senator Inouye tried to introduce the bill on the Senate side but ran into difficulty, told by the Senate parliamentarian that Senate Rule 14 prevented Congress from altering military records. Without a companion bill on the Senate side, House Resolution 3710 died with the end of the 105th Congress.

Hunter and the others regrouped to prepare for introducing differently worded legislation for the 106th Congress. Hunter had made such a good impression on the Speaker of the House that Representative Gingrich invited him to come to Washington to work for him for a summer. Hunter's dad vetoed the idea, given Hunter's age, but Hunter was allowed to spend five days in July of 1998 shadowing the Speaker, accompanying him to meetings and so on. A chance encounter in a Capitol hallway with House Whip Dick Armey resulted in Armey, the second-most powerful man in the House of Representatives, offering to have his name added to the list of the reworded legislation's sponsors.

Hunter's notoriety even landed him on *The Late Show with David Letterman* on August 6 of that year. He'd been on Letterman's show back in 1994 when he was nine, performing as part of the "Stupid Human Tricks" segment by jumping rope while bouncing on a pogo stick, so the bright lights and the cameras were familiar to him. Letterman had been impressed with Hunter the first time, and was even more respectful the second, perhaps because the talk show host had a history of taking antiauthoritarian positions, championing the little guy against the powers that be. Hunter shared the greenroom with comedian Jerry Seinfeld, who autographed a copy of *People* magazine for Hunter because they'd both been written up in it.

To keep the initiative alive and present in everybody's mind, in October Representative Scarborough submitted House Resolution 590 recognizing Hunter's efforts. It was a chance for members of Congress who'd supported the survivors to speak on the floor about the unfairness of the court-martial and the need to rectify it. Scarborough spoke on behalf of Hunter's cause, as did Representative Neil Abercrombie from Hawaii. Hunter received more press coverage afterward, and was asked by a reporter what was turning out to be an inevitable question: "What do you want to do when you grow up?"

"I want to go to the Naval Academy, and I want to be an officer," he said.

By the spring of 1999, Hunter, Monroney and the survivors had a new strategy, a pair of joint resolutions altering the language of the previous year's bill. Hunter traveled to Washington for a third time to meet with senators and congresspeople. With those already on the team, Hunter and the others discussed how the wording of the bill might be amended to make it easier for everyone to vote favorably on it. To those congresspeople he hadn't met with before, Hunter helped explain the case for exonerating McVay.

House Joint Resolution 48 was introduced on April 22, with the identical Senate Joint Resolution 26 following a month later. The resolution told the story of the sinking, the struggle in the water and the court-martial, listing all the reasons why the court-martial was unjust, and concluded by stating that it was "the sense of Congress" that the court-martial was "not morally sustainable," that the conviction of McVay was a "miscarriage of justice that led to unjust humiliation and damage to his military career," and that "the American people should now recognize Captain McVay's lack of culpability for the tragic loss." Section 2 of the resolution went on to say that it was also the sense of Congress that the final crew be awarded a Presidential Unit Citation "in recognition of the courage and fortitude displayed . . . in the face of tremendous hardship and adversity."

Representatives Scarborough from Florida and Abercrombie from Hawaii pressed the cause in the House, but the real showdown was going to come on the Senate side when Senator John Warner convened a hearing of the Senate Armed Services Committee, which he served as chairman.

The survivors had two things going for them. First, they had Senator Bob Smith, a passionate conservative from New Hampshire with a reputation for supporting oddball crusades as well as for being the nicest man in Congress. He was the son of a naval aviator who'd perished shortly after World War II when the airplane he was testing crashed. As a survivor of a naval tragedy himself, Senator Smith had thrown himself into the cause with great dedication and vigor.

The second thing the survivors had going for them was Hunter and, more germane to the hearing, the new material he was bringing with him to submit as evidence for the committee's consideration, material that people from all over the country had sent to him after seeing his name in the newspapers. He had a report entitled "ULTRA and the Sinking of the USS *Indianapolis*" sent to him by naval historian Richard A. von Doenhoff, written after von Doenhoff uncovered recently declassified documents in 1992 regarding SIGINT activities during the war. He had a letter from survivor Donald Blum stating that Thomas Brophy had used his influence to push President Truman to initiate the court-martial, something he knew because the Blums and the Brophys were longtime social acquaintances. Hunter had a letter a lawyer named Donald Koughnet had written to Kimo McVay in 1995 explaining that Captain McVay had wanted his friend Koughnet, the judge advocate for the entire western Pacific during the war, to act as his attorney at the court-martial. Koughnet's letter stated that the "brass" in Washington had interceded to deprive McVay of his choice of counsel (Captain Cady, who defended McVay, had virtually no courtroom experience) and concluded that "As a former Special Assistant to four Attorneys General of the United States, albeit years back, I am well aware of the propensity of governmental departments and agencies to appease public clamor by 'deep-sixing' loyal public servants." Hunter had a letter from Dr. Lewis Haynes, the ship's doctor, stating that after the war, when Haynes was working at the Chelsea Naval Hospital, he'd had Admiral Nimitz as a patient. Haynes had taken the opportunity to discuss the court-martial, and had heard from the lips of Admiral Nimitz himself, successor to Admiral King as chief of naval operations, that the trial should never have taken place.

Hunter even had a translation of an interview Lieutenant Commander Hashimoto, at the time a retired Shinto priest in his nineties, had given a Japanese journalist stating that he'd spoken enough English back in 1945 to know that his testimony at McVay's court-martial had been mistranslated—intentionally, it seemed to him. Because he'd been a prisoner of war in a foreign country, his protests over the mistranslation were brushed aside. Even he could see that the proceedings against McVay were contrived, Hashimoto said.

Finally, to prevail in a showdown, you need to bring your biggest guns, and Hunter had three of them, in the form of letters from men testifying that the night of the sinking, three SOS messages from the *Indianapolis* had indeed been received. The first letter came from a retiree in Sun City, Arizona, a man named Russell Hetz who'd served aboard a landing craft (LCI-1004) that had been positioned at the mouth of San Pedro Bay in the Leyte Gulf as a harbor examination vessel, tasked to keep track of ships entering and leaving the harbor. Hetz's letter stated that on the night of July 29–30, 1945, the LCI-1004 received two SOS calls from the *Indianapolis,* eight and a half minutes apart. Both messages were relayed through channels, but they were deemed by Hetz's superiors to be hoaxes, probably attempts by the Japanese to lure Allied rescue vessels into a trap, given that the radio technicians who'd received the SOS messages had been unable to get the *Indianapolis* to verify that she was sinking, and she should have verified her distress signals because nobody believed a ship the size of a heavy cruiser could sink in eight and a half minutes. Hetz added that six weeks after the sinking, "an officer with a lot of clout" came aboard the LCI-1004 and ripped a large section from the logbook, disappearing with what might have been incriminating evidence of negligence.

The second letter was from a man named Clair B. Young, a seaman who'd been on shore patrol at the naval shore facilities in Tacloban the night of the sinking. Young's letter told how he'd been standing guard at the quarters of Commodore Jacob H. Jacobson, the commandant of the base, when a messenger approached with an urgent message for the commodore that the *Indianapolis* had sent an SOS. When Young relayed the message to the groggy Jacobson and then waited for a response, Jacobson said only, "No reply at this time. If any further messages are received, notify me at once," even though of the 700 U.S. ships sunk during World War II, none had managed to send any further messages once they'd come to rest on the bottom of the sea. Young's letter also stated that when he'd awakened the commodore, he detected the "strong odor of alcohol in the room."

Most telling of all was a letter Hunter received from a Donald Allen, a retired photographer living in New Hampshire. He'd worked the midnight to 8 A.M. watch at Tacloban as a driver for the Philippine Sea Frontier's commander, Commodore Norman C. Gillette. On the night of the sinking, Gillette had been playing bridge at a base in Guiwan, ninety miles up the shore from Tacloban, leaving Allen free to stand watch that night in the officer of the day's office. While he was there, a technician from the radio shack located in the back half of the Quonset hut burst in, ashen-faced, and said he'd received an SOS from the *Indianapolis,* clear as a bell, with coordinates, saying she'd been torpedoed and was sinking. They immediately summoned the officer on duty, Lieutenant Gibson, who double-checked to make sure the distress call was for real. Gibson then dispatched two seagoing tugs to the coordinates given, powerful stubby vessels with mighty engines capable of thirty knots.

Allen finished his duty, went to bed and woke up curious to hear what had happened to the *Indianapolis.* When he asked, he was told that Gillette had become furious that a subordinate officer had dispatched ships without his permission and actually ordered the tugs to turn around and return to base, simply because he hadn't been the one who sent them. In a follow-up letter to Hunter Scott, Allen alleged that a cover-up had taken place at the naval shore facilities at Tacloban. Considering that both Gillette and Gibson were questioned in the inquiry that followed the disaster, if what Allen was saying was true, then the navy had even more to answer for than anyone had previously known. If those tugs had been allowed to proceed, hundreds of sailors on the *Indianapolis* might have been saved.

Chapter Thirteen

The Reckoning
September 14, 1999

Men and nations behave wisely once they have exhausted the alternatives.

Abba Eban

The Senate Armed Services Committee hearing was called to order the morning of Tuesday, September 14, 1999. The day before, Hunter had been elected president of his freshman class at Pensacola High School. He was missing two football practices, and his coach told him if he missed practice, he wouldn't start, but Hunter knew he was involved in something considerably more important than the game on Friday. Among the eleven survivors who'd come to Washington at their own expense to honor their captain were Giles McCoy, Harlan Twible, Mike Kuryla, Robert McGuiggan and Jack Miner. The survivors wore blue jackets with a picture of the ship on the back, above the ship a row of ten stars for the ten battles the *Indianapolis* had fought in, beneath the ship the hull number, CA-35, and the inscription "Still at Sea." The survivors also wore blue baseball-style caps decorated with gold brocade, their individual medals pinned to their caps, with the picture of the ship on the front, and on the back, an arc of yellow lettering that read "Survivor." Wives and family members attended the hearing as well. The room was packed with photographers and reporters, a video and a film crew positioned to record the event. The panelists waiting to testify sat in front, below the elevated seats where the senators would preside.

Sitting across the aisle from the survivors, representing the navy, was Admiral Donald Pilling, vice chief of naval operations, the number two man in the navy, whose presence surprised the survivors. They hadn't expected anyone of such high rank. Joining Pilling were Rear Admiral John D. Hutson, judge advocate general of the navy, and Dr. William S. Dudley, director of naval history. There was a support contingent of officers both in suits and in uniform, as well as a handful of cadets, about twenty all together.

When Senator Bob Smith entered the hearing room, heads turned. He was a tall, vigorous man of considerable presence, and it seemed clear to Hunter by the way Smith walked that he was primed and ready for the contest. Hunter and Monroney had met with Smith in Smith's office before the hearing to go over what to say. They also talked about what to expect from the navy—intransigence and obduracy, mostly. Senator John Warner, chairman of the Senate Armed Services Committee and former secretary of the navy, was last to arrive. No one had told Hunter, but the fear was that Warner had only called the meeting to silence them once and for all. Nor was Hunter aware that lobbyist Mike Monroney believed Warner was convening the hearing only as a favor to his friend Senator Smith.

"We are here to remember the sinking of the USS *Indianapolis*," Warner said in his opening remarks, "but more significantly to remember the courage of those who were aboard the ship that fateful night, and particularly those who are here with us today. . . ."

Warner then introduced Senator Smith, seated to his left. Smith's remarks were more to the point. "This was one of the greatest tragedies in

U.S. naval history, the sinking of the USS *Indianapolis*," he said. "Today we have before us a number of the survivors of this tragedy. I think it might be appropriate when we introduce the witnesses, Mr. Chairman, to introduce those gentlemen who are here today. In the sinking of the USS *Indianapolis,* the ship lost eight hundred eighty crew members. We're here today to honor both the memory of the sailors who lost their lives, but also those brave souls who survived. The courage of the crew of the USS *Indianapolis* is incredible. It shines like a beacon even decades later. Today the committee will have the privilege of hearing this story from some of those who lived through it. There's a great history here. . . ."

For the next twenty minutes, Smith told the story of how the *Indianapolis* delivered the bomb, and how she was sunk just after midnight, July 30, 1945. It was a story most of the people in the room were familiar with, but Smith was speaking for the historical record now. He talked of Captain McVay's exemplary career, and how he'd been awarded the Silver Star for courage under fire during the Solomon Islands campaign.

"This was a good captain," Smith said. "He was a good sailor. He did his job. Much better than some others who came back." Smith described how both Admiral Nimitz and Admiral Spruance had recommended against a court-martial, only to be overruled by Admiral King. He described how Secretary of the Navy Forrestal had remitted the sentence afterward, which could, he said, be interpreted as an admission that the trial had been unjust.

"New information has surfaced raising significant questions about the justice of his conviction," Smith concluded, "and I just want to say at this point, Mr. Chairman, I am not a historical revisionist. I deplore it. Questioning whether it was morally right to have Captain McVay court-martialed in the first place is what we're doing. That isn't revisionism. That's trying to set the record straight. This past spring, I had the good fortune of meeting with Hunter Scott and survivors of the USS *Indianapolis*. Meeting these gentlemen in person was a very emotional experience. These men are not historical revisionists. They lost comrades. They would have no problem in saying so if their captain caused the death of their comrades." Smith acknowledged that the case of the USS *Indianapolis* and Captain McVay had been investigated before. "However," he said, "because of the efforts of some of our witnesses today, the survivors' group, and in particular Hunter Scott, of Pensacola, Florida, I think new information has been brought to light, and I would ask this committee and the Senate to listen very carefully to that testimony. It is new information that was not available at the time of the court-martial and indeed I believe it is new information that was not available in the investigations that subsequently followed."

When Senator Warner invited the survivors present to introduce themselves, they stood, one by one, and spoke. Some were nervous about being in such a grandly appointed Senate hearing room with television cameras recording their words, and found it difficult to speak. Some fought back tears, thinking back fifty-five years, remembering the dead, and they felt honored to testify at last on their behalf.

"My name is Harlan Twible, and I served as an ensign aboard the USS *Indianapolis.*"

"I'm Giles McCoy, from Florida, and I was a PFC from the Marine Corps aboard the *Indianapolis.* We had thirty-nine marines aboard, and we did the security duty aboard ship."

"I'm Bob McGuiggan. I was a gunner's mate striker, Fourth Division, on the five-inch, and a catapult gunner's mate. I came aboard the *Indianapolis* in forty-two, and spent nine invasion operations with the *Indianapolis.*"

"Mike Kuryla, junior. I was a coxswain aboard the ship, Fourth Division, fourth section, the five-inch twenty-fives. I was director of fire control."

"My name is Jack Miner, from Northbrook, Illinois. I was a radio technician, second class." He paused, and then said, "My time aboard ship was two weeks. That's all of it."

Each survivor had a statement he'd prepared to read into the congressional record, but before they did, Hunter gave an introduction. If the legislative process was a labyrinthine video game like Myst or Dungeons and Dragons, Hunter knew he was at the final level, loaded with ammunition and at the top of his game. He'd been answering these questions for three years. There was nothing they could throw at him that he wasn't ready for, no question he didn't know the answer to—this was what they'd been building toward ever since he'd first started his history fair project, the point of all the work he'd done.

"My journey to this committee as witness began over three years ago," Hunter said, "when I saw the motion picture *Jaws,* in which an actor described in chilling detail how he and the other survivors floated for five days in shark-infested waters before they were spotted by accident and rescued. I asked my dad if the story was true, and he said it was, and suggested I research the story for a sixth-grade history fair project. I found little information about the *Indianapolis* in history books. I put an ad in our local navy newspaper, asking for information about survivors of the *Indianapolis.* A call led me to Mr. Maurice Glenn Bell, a survivor, who lives in Mobile, Alabama. In the fall of 1996, I met with Mr. Bell and I heard the *Indianapolis* story firsthand. The story was as chilling as the story in *Jaws.* Mr. Bell gave me a list of all remaining one hundred and fifty-four survivors of the *Indianapolis.* And over the course of the next year, I called and wrote every one of them. Over eighty responded to my request for information, and filled out a questionnaire I sent them. One of the questions was whether or not they felt Captain McVay's court-martial was justified and his conviction was fair.

"All of the responses I got back were unanimous, and most were strongly worded in outrage and anger over the court-martial and conviction of their captain. It seemed to me that after doing so much to help shorten the war, and after the nightmare of his ship being lost and his crew being killed and drowned around him, and his own struggle for survival for days in the open sea, that somehow the court-martial of Captain McVay was not right.

"Abraham Lincoln once said, 'The probability that we may fail in a struggle ought not to deter us from a cause we believe to be just.' I know you are here today because you believe deeply in American democracy and in the fact that you can make a difference for the constituents you represent. I am no different than you in this belief, and that is why I have journeyed here, as a representative for my heroes, the men of the *Indianapolis*. I have learned that democracy is a treasure so valued, men and women are willing to give their lives in its pursuit. I know eight hundred eighty men of the USS *Indianapolis* made the supreme sacrifice. I pray that some of those who gave their lives are looking down on what I'm doing at this moment with a smile, knowing their sacrifice was not in vain."

Hunter then held up the set of dog tags that had belonged to Captain McVay, given to him by McVay's son Kimo.

"I carry this as a reminder of my mission and in memory of the man who ended his own life in 1968. I carry this to remind me that only in the United States can one person make a difference, no matter what the age. I carry this dog tag to remind me of the privilege and responsibility I have to carry forward the torch of honor, passed to me by the men of the USS *Indianapolis*. In 1806 Thomas Jefferson wrote, 'Political interest can never be separated in the long run from moral right.' Fifty-four years after the court-martial of a man who should never have been brought to trial, we are now in the 'long run,' and you have the opportunity to do what is morally right. You can set the historical record straight concerning Captain McVay and the crew of the USS *Indianapolis*. When I started this mission there were a hundred and fifty-four survivors. Today there are a hundred and thirty-four still with us. Please honor these men with the passage of Senate Resolution twenty-six. Please restore the honor of their ship, while some of these men are still alive to see this dream become a reality. Please do not forget about the men of the USS *Indianapolis* for the second time in fifty-four years."

As Hunter recited his statement, it seemed clear to some observers that Senator Warner's interest sharpened. He leaned forward in his seat, listening intently. Warner's interest was whetted further when the survivors submitted their statements, telling their personal stories. Twible stood and talked about how dark it was the night the ship was torpedoed, and how ludicrous it was to think McVay could have passed the word to abandon ship with all communications out. McCoy stood and spoke of the efforts over the years by the survivors to clear their captain's name. After the statements were read, Senator Smith began a cross-examination.

"Now, Mr. Scott," he began. "I know that in your research you found some documents that had not been found before. I want to ask you about one of them, the so-called ULTRA document, about breaking the code. Can you elaborate just briefly on what that was and also indicate to the committee why that's significant?"

Hunter was only too happy to comply. He knew the facts cold, and didn't need to so much as glance at his notes.

"So it is correct then," Smith said when Hunter was finished, "that this information, because of the classification level, was not brought into the court-martial. Is that correct?"

"Yes, sir," Hunter said.

Smith asked, "Do we have it on record that Captain McVay specifically asked for an escort ship?"

Hunter said he did, and explained how it was that the *Indianapolis* sailed with neither an escort nor antisubmarine warfare equipment. He helped explain why the ship wasn't reported overdue. Finally, Smith asked about the documents Hunter had presented the committee regarding SOS messages received and ignored. "This also was not introduced at the court-martial, is that correct?"

"Yes, sir," Hunter answered. "The official navy version states that no SOS messages were received, but through my research, I've found that to be false. They were received in three different places."

"Where did you find this in your research, Hunter?" Smith asked.

"After I appeared on various shows, people would call me up. I received a call from Mr. Russell Hetz, saying he received an SOS message. He was aboard the LCI-1004 harbor examination vessel in Leyte Gulf when a message came in. And then they got another one, eight and a half minutes later. They said a ship of that size could not sink that fast, and it was regarded as a prank call from the Japanese to lure rescue vessels in the area. Also there was another one received, by Mr. Clair B. Young. Mr. Young says he received the SOS and reported it to his boss, who was drunk at the time. His boss said, 'No reply at this time, if any further messages come, notify me at once.' But no further messages came. The third place it was received was by Mr. Don Allen. Mr. Allen received it, and the guy in charge there had orders not to be disturbed, because he was playing cards. So they took some initiative and sent out two seagoing tugs to the area where the *Indianapolis* was. And when the admiral was done playing cards—I'm sorry, *Commodore* Gillette—when he was notified, he made the tugs turn around, because he did not send them out."

"It's my understanding," Smith said, "that this information was not available at the time of the court-martial and was not part of the court-martial, is that correct?"

"That is correct," Hunter said.

"Part of the testimony that came out in the trial, correct me if I'm wrong, was that there was no SOS sent. Is that correct?" Senator Smith asked. "That nothing was received from McVay?"

"That is correct," Hunter Scott answered.

"That's pretty dramatic new information," Senator Smith said.

Hunter felt satisfied with how the proceedings were going so far, but he knew that the other side had yet to speak. Senator Smith turned to the navy panel and asked them to give their prepared statements. Dr. Dudley admitted that the *Indianapolis* had been deprived of the intelligence available at the time. He stated that the transmission and receipt of SOS messages remained a matter of controversy. Rear Admiral Hutson, the navy's chief legal officer, spoke to the legality of the McVay court-martial, and how a court of inquiry had placed "serious blame" on Captain McVay for his failure to zigzag. McVay had been appointed counsel and was given the opportunity to examine witnesses and present evidence, ably represented by a navy captain with two lieutenants as assistant defense counsel, Hutson said. He referred to the remitted sentence. "I personally read the entire record of trial," Hutson closed, "and I conclude that the proceedings were fair and provided full due process of law. Admiral McVay had every right applicable to trial by court-martial. The record clearly indicates that Admiral McVay's counsel performed his duties well."

Hutson's final words expressed the gist of the navy's position on the matter.

"There is a popular misconception," Hutson said, "that Captain McVay was brought to trial for losing his ship in combat. In fact, the loss of the ship was not an element of either of the two charges referred against Captain McVay. The loss of the ship was legally irrelevant to the proof of the prosecution's case."

Admiral Pilling gave the final statement and reiterated the navy's position. He was a former destroyer commander. He'd been a member of the National Security Council and a fellow at the Brookings Institution, and had received a Defense Distinguished Service Medal, among many other awards. Trim and gray-haired, scholarly in manner, he spoke precisely and forthrightly. He explained the principles of authority and accountability in the navy, stating that a commanding officer has full authority and full accountability for his ship and crew, and that there is no parallel for the principle of accountability in the command of a ship, either in civilian life or in other parts of the military.

"Captain McVay understood these concepts perfectly. . . . Such a disaster as that of the USS *Indianapolis* would be investigated, and over the course of the fifty-four years since it happened, it has been reexamined. Several analyses by navy experts and independent analyses have all pronounced the proceedings of the court-martial as fair. I personally am confident that the court-martial was legal and fair. It is an important distinction that the charge and conviction did not attribute the loss of the *Indianapolis* to McVay's actions. While the ship's loss undeniably brought the harsh spotlight of accountability on the commanding officer's actions, the court-martial did not find that those actions caused the loss of the ship. . . . Captain McVay had absolute accountability for his decisions and actions. When those decisions were examined by court-martial of experienced officers, Captain McVay was found guilty of an error in professional judgment. I firmly believe that his trial was fair."

Senator Smith immediately picked up on the two feeblest parts of the navy's argument. First, a law is not fair if it's unequally applied—you can put together rock-solid evidence to prove and convict a man of jaywalking, but if you have the same amount of rock-solid evidence against a second man, but choose not to enforce the law against him, then the conviction of the first man is unfair, no matter how many lawyers he has or how legally conducted the trial was. Second, the contention that the loss of the ship had nothing to do with the conviction was, simply, preposterous doublespeak, and Smith wanted to point out that it was. Hunter sat back and listened, gratified. At last, somebody was asking the navy the questions that needed to be asked. He felt sorry for Admiral Pilling because he seemed like someone being quizzed in front of a class who wished he'd had a few more days to study.

"In reading your statement, Admiral Pilling," Smith said, sighing, his hands first touching his eyebrows and then flaring upward. "It's weak." Admiral Pilling flinched slightly, then looked at his papers. "Not the statement, but the court-martial. Let me just recap here. There were hundreds of American ships sunk out there in the water. Nobody was court-martialed for the sinking of a ship other than Captain McVay. You had Admiral Nimitz and Admiral Spruance both recommend no on the court-martial. They were the superior officers in the region. Based on your own testimony," Smith said, his voice rising, "you're saying it was a judgment that they court-martialed him for. Not to zigzag. Not for the sinking of the ship. You've got the Japanese commander of the submarine that sunk the ship testify at the court-martial, that 'I popped up with my periscope, and I sunk him, zigzagging would not have made a difference.' So let me ask you a point-blank direct question." Smith's hands chopped the air with each syllable. "Was McVay—to blame—for the sinking—the sinking—of the USS *Indianapolis*? Was he? Yes or no?"

Admiral Pilling leaned to the microphone. "As I said in my statement, sir, he was not tried for the sinking."

"That's what I understand," Smith said. "So if he was not tried and court-martialed for the sinking of the ship, then he was court-martialed for a judgment that he made, not to zigzag. Even though we had testimony saying that it was questionable. It was his prerogative, we understand that. At best we can say the weather was clear as a bell. At worst we can say it wasn't clear. We had the officer on duty saying he couldn't see to the other end of the ship."

Smith was on a roll now, his speech quickening.

"So we now are in a situation where no other captain had been court-martialed. I mean, did we go through and review, whatever—seven hundred, I don't know what the number was, but if it was seven hundred ships that were sunk—did we look at every single one of those sinkings, and look at the judgment of those captains prior to that? Did we analyze every one of those and say, 'Well, he didn't zigzag, he didn't zag that, he didn't know this, he didn't know that?' I don't think we did. . . . It's to me bizarre," Smith said, folding his hands in toward his heart, "that one individual would be court-martialed on a judgment." His brow furrowed, Smith asked, "Would any of you men wearing the uniform like to be court-martialed on an error in judgment? That had no direct impact on the loss of lives? How would you feel if that were your son, or you?"

Admiral Pilling pointed out that although Admiral Nimitz said that McVay shouldn't go to court-martial, Nimitz did recommend that McVay should receive a letter of reprimand for his error in judgment.

"That's a big difference," Smith said, using an index finger to keep the beat. "Let's face it. Big difference between a letter of reprimand and a court-martial. And you said that the navy had a number of weaknesses. That's the term you used."

"Right," Admiral Pilling said.

"In the way they noted and tracked ships, and weaknesses in survival equipment on board. But it's interesting that when the navy talks about their mistakes, they're not mistakes, they're weaknesses. When we talk about possible mistakes by Captain McVay, it's a court-martial offense."

Smith asked Hutson if there were any other court-martials—if the commodore who allegedly received the SOS was court-martialed. Hutson replied that no, there were no other court-martials.

"I think we're looking at a court-martial which is very technical in wording," Smith said. "Captain McVay was court-martialed for an error in judgment. There's a technical point here, that Captain McVay was not culpable for the loss of the *Indianapolis* and its crew. Do you agree with that statement, all of you?"

"What I said was that the court did not find him culpable," Admiral Pilling replied.

"Right," Smith said, leaning forward and seeming to grow larger. "But the *perception* is that they did."

"That's true," Senator Warner added.

"The *perception*," Smith continued, "is that the man was court-martialed because the ship went down and twelve hundred sailors went into the water. That's clearly the perception. And frankly, I think you have to ask yourself, honestly, if the incident had not occurred, and the ship had not sunk, and Captain McVay had entered port into Leyte, would he have been court-martialed?"

"We wouldn't know," Pilling said weakly.

"I think you can conclude," Smith pressed, "that it would be pretty ridiculous to single out a captain, with a reputation that he had, and court-martial him if that ship went on to port safely. . . . How can you say that he didn't cause the sinking of the ship, and then say that it's morally sustainable to court-martial him? Can you say that it was not unjust humiliation and damage to his naval career if he did not cause the sinking of the ship? You know full well that he would not have been court-martialed if the ship had not been sunk. So to draw these kinds of silly technical points in the court-martial, if everybody in America today and everybody in America then—and by the way, the American public was not notified for two or three weeks after the sinking that it happened, including the families—we all know what the perception is." Smith shook his head incredulously. "I've looked at cases like this before, and I've come down on the side of the navy many times, as the navy people here know. Guys, I'm trying to be objective, but this simply is not right. It's just not right."

Admiral Pilling tried to respond by repeating that the penalties imposed on Captain McVay were trivial. Senator Warner stopped him short, indicating that by the presence of the survivors in the hearing room, and their testimony, and their efforts over the years, something more than trivial was going on. Smith held up two closed fists, opened them wide and made his point again.

"There is an inconsistency here. If you're going to use the principles of accountability, then you have to apply them to all officers who are involved. You did not do that. What I'm saying to you is," Smith said, punctuating with a thumb and forefinger, "if you're going to do this to one man who was involved in this incident, you've got to do it to everybody. And you didn't do that, which is what makes the court-martial, in my opinion, morally wrong."

"That's a key question," Senator Warner agreed.

Smith repeated that there would have been no trial had the *Indianapolis* sailed safely into Leyte.

"Suppose all eleven hundred ninety-seven men came into port alive. The ship is in good shape. No four days of shark attacks, no exposure to weather and the water. No fires. No botched search. No botched recovery effort. No botched withholding of evidence. No ignoring of enemy message traffic. And upon arrival of the crew, and the ship, one of these men, or one of their colleagues, made a request to the navy that said, Captain McVay did not zigzag. . . ."

Smith paused for a moment.

"You're telling me he would have been court-martialed?"

Muffled laughter rose.

"There is no way. And you know it. And if he wasn't gonna be court-martialed then, you made a mistake. And if you tell me that he caused the deaths of those men, then okay, I might disagree with you, but at least you can say the court-martial was justified, but you can't court-martial somebody for a judgment, and then not court-martial everybody else who made errors in judgment, that cost the lives of more men. And you didn't do it." Smith turned his hands palms up. "That's why there's an injustice here. We should change injustices. Not rewrite history, but change injustices. The man wore the uniform, just like you wore it. And he wore it proudly. And he was one hell of an officer. And he would not have been given that bomb to take to the *Enola Gay* if he wasn't. And I think he endured punishment that none of us could ever understand, probably, and he paid the ultimate price for it. And we have a chance that he'll never know about, to make it right. Not to overturn the court-martial, just to simply say a mistake was made."

After Smith finished speaking, Senator Warner confessed that the new evidence and the testimony of Hunter Scott and of the survivors had changed his mind, "righted his course," his use of a navy term. He was on the side of the *Indianapolis* now.

Chapter Fourteen

The Exoneration
October 12, 2000, to July 11, 2001

Let them in, Peter, they are very tired;
Give them the couches where the angels sleep.
Let them wake whole again to new dawns fired
With sun not war. And may their peace be deep.
Remember where the broken bodies lie . . . And give them things they like.
Let them make noise.
God knows how young they were to have to die!
Give swing bands, not gold harps, to these our boys.
Let them love, Peter, — they have had no time —
Girls sweet as meadow wind with flowering hair . . .
They should have trees and bird songs, hills to climb —
The taste of summer in a ripened pear. Tell them
How they are missed. Say not to fear;
It's going to be all right with us down here.

Elma Dean, "Letter to St. Peter"

In a distant foreign port, a United States destroyer rested in a harbor. On deck, sailors went about their business, cleaning what needed to be cleaned, stowing away what needed to be stowed away, reading manuals, doing paperwork, talking about how they hoped they'd be home for Thanksgiving, and whether or not there was going to be a subway series between the Yankees and the Mets. Below, skipping across a calm sea, two men approached in a small rubber Zodiac, possibly a delivery of some sort, judging by the boxes visible on the floor of the motorized raft. When the Zodiac reached the side of the destroyer, there was a massive explosion, obliterating the men in the Zodiac and leaving a hole in the hull of the ship forty feet across. On board, seventeen American sailors were dead and thirty-nine were injured. The ship was the USS *Cole,* and the port was Aden, Yemen. The date was October 12, 2000.

That same day in Washington, D.C., the Senate passed Joint Resolution 26. House Joint Resolution 48 had been passed earlier in the week. The resolution was attached to a defense appropriations bill, and in its final language it read, after a brief description of the facts of the case, that it was the sense of Congress that:

> (1) in light of the remission by the Secretary of the Navy of the sentence of the court-martial and the restoration of Captain McVay to active duty by the Chief of Naval Operations, Fleet Admiral Chester Nimitz, that the American people should now recognize Captain McVay's lack of culpability for the tragic loss of the USS *Indianapolis* and the lives of the men who died as a result of the sinking of that vessel; and

> (2) in light of the fact that certain exculpatory information was not available to the court-martial board

and that Captain McVay's conviction resulted therefrom, that Captain McVay's military record should now reflect that he is exonerated for the loss of the USS *Indianapolis* and so many of her crew.

In January of 2001, Admiral Robert J. Natter, in charge of investigating the bombing of the USS *Cole,* ruled that *Cole* skipper Commander Kirk S. Lippold could have done sixty-two things to protect his ship from terrorist attacks but only implemented thirty-two of those precautions. All the same, Natter recommended that no one be punished because Lippold "acted correctly, given the information that was made available to him." According to Admiral Vernon Clark, the chief of naval operations, "The investigation clearly shows that the commanding officer of the *Cole* did not have the specific intelligence, focused training, appropriate equipment or on-scene security support to effectively prevent or deter such a determined, planned assault on his ship. In short, the system—all of us—did not equip this skipper for success in the environment he encountered in Aden harbor that fateful day." In the aftermath, the chairman of the Joint Chiefs of Staff himself, General Henry Shelton, promised to look into why "the *Cole* was sent alone into the harbor of a Middle Eastern nation known as the center of terrorist activity at a time when the region was in crisis."

This may be part of the legacy of Hunter Scott's efforts to clear Captain McVay's record, the notion that accountability extends beyond the captain of a ship to include his immediate superiors.

When the September 1999 Senate Armed Services Committee hearing was over, panelists on the *Indianapolis* side stood and shook hands and hugged one another. Hunter had a feeling of triumph, even though he was disappointed that the navy hadn't admitted they'd made a mistake despite the overwhelming evidence. The important thing was that they'd persuaded Senator Warner. The survivors posed for a group photograph, with Hunter and Senator Smith in the middle. Smith congratulated everyone on a job well done. Jack Miner had tears in his eyes, and told Hunter that until he'd seen the letters Hunter had compiled, he'd never known anyone had heard the SOS he'd helped send. His tears came from remembering the heroism of the men in the water, and of guys like Chief Woods, sending his SOS until the very last minute, telling young sailors like Miner who were too scared to think straight that they needed to get their life jackets on and abandon ship—taking care of others, without regard to his own safety.

Admiral Pilling looked a bit stunned when the hearing was over, sandbagged and blindsided, as if he'd also expected Senator Warner to bury the issue once and for all, only to find himself on the hot seat. He'd been through a "murder board" before the hearing, a mock interrogation where his assistants threw every hard question they could think of at him, but all the same, he came off seeming unprepared. Hunter Scott had the same impression, and even went so far as to approach the admiral as he was talking to his staff and say, respectfully, "Excuse me, sir—I'd like to give you a copy of my research, because it appeared you had some difficulty answering some of the questions, and I think this will provide you with some of the answers." Pilling turned, took the packet Hunter offered him and muttered a quiet "Thank you," then turned back to his staff, displeased, the expression on his face seemed to say, at being shown up by a kid. He was a brilliant man, with a Ph.D. in mathematics from Cambridge, and probably wasn't used to having teenagers offer to help him answer questions.

Many wondered afterward what harm there would be in the navy's admitting it had made a mistake in court-martialing McVay. To be fair, the navy had investigated itself over the years and had owned up to virtually every mistake it had made regarding the disaster. The difference, as Senator Smith so eloquently pointed out, was in the degree of punishment and the disproportionate suffering it caused. Smith wanted to know—would the navy have court-martialed McVay if the ship hadn't sunk? Of course not. Perhaps the navy's obstinacy over the last thirty years stemmed from a sense that Congress would never have re-examined the court-martial if McVay hadn't committed suicide, and that wasn't the navy's fault.

Would Hunter Scott still have been motivated to clear McVay's name if the captain hadn't committed suicide? Absolutely. Hunter Scott is, by most measures, a normal kid. What makes him a bit different from a lot of kids may be his extremely well-defined sense of right and wrong, a sense springing from his deeply held religious beliefs.

That is unlikely to change. Many things about Hunter did change during his crusade to help the survivors of the *Indianapolis*. The little boy is now over six feet tall, his sweet small voice today deep and adult-sounding, though still full of polite "yes, sirs" and "no, ma'ams." His boyish shyness has been replaced by a quiet confidence, though his innate curiosity is intact. His goals have changed too. When he started, he thought he wanted to join the navy when he grew up, but after seeing how the navy bullies people, he's not so sure anymore. Lately the Coast Guard has been looking better and better.

After the 1999 hearing, the survivors went home and got on with their lives. They visited with their grandchildren, watched the news on television, stayed in touch with each other via e-mail, and waited. When the resolution passed in October of 2000, they celebrated a significant victory, but they still wanted to know what action the navy was going to take—if any. Years of frustration prevented them from feeling too optimistic.

In the fall of 2000, George W. Bush was elected President of the United States. Florida Representative Joe Scarborough offered to set up a meeting between Hunter and President Bush, at which time Hunter could petition the president to expunge all mention of the court-martial from Captain McVay's records. Hunter waited to hear from Scarborough. Then on April 18, 2001, the navy sent Senators Warner and Smith a letter indicating their desire to comply with the legislation passed the previous October. On April 24, 2001, President Bush nominated Gordon R. England to be his new secretary of the navy. Three days later, the navy announced it would offer the crew of the *Indianapolis* a Navy Unit Citation, and that it would retrieve Captain McVay's record from the National Personnel Records Center in St. Louis for review to "determine the best approach to modify his record." In June, a month after he was sworn in, Secretary of the Navy England met with Senator Smith to discuss McVay's case. On July 11, England sent Smith a letter stating that although he did not have the legal authority to overturn a court-martial or delete the findings from McVay's record, he did have the power to insert a copy of the Senate Resolution into Captain McVay's file, thus addressing the false perception that McVay was responsible for the tragedy.

Hunter was fishing in the pond in his backyard when Mike Monroney phoned him with the news of McVay's exoneration. The exhilaration lasted for days, kept alive each time a survivor called or wrote to thank Hunter for his efforts on their behalf.

By the time this book comes out, Hunter will be as old as some of the men who enlisted and went off to fight the Japanese and the Germans, over half a century ago, just a bunch of boys, doing their duty for their country, cocky young guys who believed they were going to live forever. By the time this book comes out, more of the survivors will have died. Each will have found his own way to peace. Someday, in the not-so-distant future, there will only be a handful left, enough to fill a small life raft, and then there will be a mere half dozen, and then five, then four, then three, then two, then one, and then there will only be the story of what happened to them, the record, which a young boy helped set straight.

Acknowledgments

First and foremost I'd like to thank Hunter Scott and his family, father Alan, mother Leslie and sister Whitney, for furnishing me with books, articles, newspaper clippings and videotapes, for answering my questions and e-mails, and for welcoming me to Florida and spending time with me there. Many of the resource materials for this book, both primary and background, were originally amassed by Hunter in his quest to exonerate Captain McVay, including letters and relevant articles from the survivors themselves, to the extent that Hunter Scott now probably has more information on the USS *Indianapolis* in his private collection than any government archive or public library. What they sent was nearly overwhelming, and I'm sure it wasn't half of all they had. I couldn't have wished for greater cooperation and assistance, and I join with the survivors in thanking Hunter Scott for all the work he's done. He is a remarkable young man and I suspect we have not heard the last of him.

Among the survivors who spoke with me both on and off the record, I am most grateful to Maurice Bell, Mike Kuryla, Giles McCoy,

Robert McGuiggan, Jack Miner, Morgan Moseley and Harlan Twible, not only for helping me with my research but also for fighting for this country over fifty years ago. I know that for all my efforts to imagine what they went through and to reproduce and illustrate their experiences in this book, words will never completely convey the full measure of their suffering or adequately illuminate the sacrifices they made in the defense of freedom. They are not men who have ever sought personal glory or attention, and most will tell you they were only doing their job, only doing what they had to do, and no better than anybody else, but they are heroes all the same. Particular thanks to Diane Smith for sending a personal narrative written by her late husband, Cozell, that he'd entitled "For Peace of Mind." The first chapter of this book is an account based on that narrative, drawn to approximate his experience aided by information given to me by Diane and by Cozell's son Michael. Thanks as well to Mrs. Katherine Moore, whose beloved husband, K.C., went down on the *Indianapolis* and who reminded me that the families of the men who died are also survivors and should never be forgotten.

Thanks to Don Allen in New Hampshire and to Mako Hanyu in Japan, to Professor Jaimie Hubbard in the Asian Studies department at Smith College in Northampton, Massachusetts, and thanks to Shawn Lindholm at the University of Massachusetts Translation Center in Amherst. Thanks to Dennis Bilger, archivist at the Truman Library, and to George Burgess, director of the International Shark Attack File and the coordinator of museum operations at the Florida Museum of Natural History in Gainesville, Florida. Thanks also to Dr. Lisa Natanson at the National Oceanic and Atmospheric Administration, and to Carol Coon at the San Francisco Public Library. Thanks and appreciation to Dr. Al Steinman, one of the foremost authorities on survival at sea and former head of the United States Coast Guard's medical program. Thanks to Hugh O'Doherty, former Coast Guard pilot, for edifying me as to search and rescue at sea, and to Captain William J. Toti, former commander of the nuclear submarine USS *Indianapolis,* whose firsthand knowledge of the responsibilities of command proved invaluable to me. Also a very special thanks to Senator Robert Smith of New

Hampshire for giving me so much of his time on the phone (proof that he may be, as one D.C. insider told me, "the nicest man in Washington") and for having the wisdom to listen to a little boy, and thanks to retired lobbyist Mike Monroney for helping me understand how Washington works—his efforts on behalf of the survivors would make for another entire book, though for editorial purposes they have been given only a passing mention here.

I'd like to thank my intrepid researchers Dave Hower and Mark Erelli for both finding the answers to my questions and supplying me with the answers to questions I forgot to ask. Thanks as well to Lisa Timmons, the best travel agent in America, at United Nations Travel in Philadelphia.

On the publishing side, thanks to editor Karen Wojtyla for the great job she did of reducing my original text to a more manageable length and keeping things moving, and thanks to Beverly Horowitz for bringing her vision to the project. Much thanks to Doug Whynott, a great writer who initially got this book off the ground, and even more thanks to my agent, Todd Shuster, for originally recognizing what a great story we had and for his inspired creativity during the process of drafting and selling the proposal to the right people in the right way.

Finally, thanks to my wife, Jennifer Gates, for all her support and understanding during the drawn-out writing process and for taking the baby those times when I needed both hands to write. Thanks also to Jack for helping me by sitting on my lap, which taught me to type fairly quickly with only one hand.

Bibliography

"For the Good of the Navy." *Insight Magazine,* 5 June 2000.

Anderson, Jim. "The Tragic *Indianapolis* Story Told." NCVA *Cryptolog,* Spring 1984.

Bartholomew, Robert E., and Erich Goode. "Mass Delusions and Hysterias: Highlights from the Past Millennium." *Skeptical Inquirer,* May 2000.

Bondi, Victor, ed. *American Decades.* Detroit: Thompson, 1995.

Buell, Thomas. *Master of Seapower: The Biography of Fleet Admiral Ernest J. King.* Annapolis, Md.: Naval Institute Press, 1995.

Cady, Capt. John. Transcript of summary at court-martial. December 1945.

Carey, F. G., and J. V. Scharold. "Movement of Blue Sharks in Depth and Course." *Marine Biology,* 1990, 106.

Collier, Richard. *The Road to Pearl Harbor: 1941.* New York: Atheneum, 1981.

Compagno, Leonard J. V., ed. *Sharks of the World, FAO Species Catalogue, vol. 4.* Rome: United Nations Development Program, 1984.

Dean, Elma. "Letter to St. Peter." *American Mercury Magazine,* November 1942.

Dew, Gwen. "Horrors in Hong Kong." *American Mercury Magazine,* November 1942.

Dudley, Dr. William S. Congressional statement. 14 September 1999.

Embree, Ainsley T., ed. *Encyclopedia of Asian History.* New York: Scribner, 1988.

Ethridge, Kenneth E. "The Agony of the *Indianapolis.*" *American Heritage,* August–September 1982, 33, no. 5.

Forrestal, V. Adm. E. P. *Admiral Raymond Spruance, USN: A Study in Command.* Washington: Government Printing Office, 1966.

Foulkes, David. *The Psychology of Sleep.* New York: Scribner, 1966.

Gackenbach, Jayne, and Stephen LaBerge, eds. *Conscious Mind, Sleeping Brain: Perspectives on Lucid Dreaming.* New York: Plenum Press, 1988.

Gilbert, Perry W., ed. *Sharks and Survival.* Boston: D.C. Heath and Co., 1963.

Hashimoto, Mochitsura. *Sunk: The Story of the Japanese Submarine Fleet, 1941–1945.* New York, Henry Holt, 1954.

Haynes, Dr. Lewis L., and George W. Campbell. "We Prayed While 883 Died." *Saturday Evening Post,* 6 August 1955.

———"Survivor of the *Indianapolis.*" *Navy Medicine Magazine* (no date).

Herman, Dr. Judith. *Trauma and Recovery.* New York: Basic Books, 1992.

Hinshaw, David. *The Home Front.* New York: Putnam, 1943.

Hutson, R. Adm. John. Congressional statement. 14 September 1999.

Kandel, Dr. Eric R., and Dr. James H. Schwartz. *Principles of Neural Science.* New York: Elsevier, 1991.

Kuryla, Mike. Congressional statement. 14 September 1999.

Kurzman, Dan. "Four Nights of Terror." *American Legion Magazine,* August 1981.

————*Fatal Voyage: The Sinking of the USS* Indianapolis. New York: Atheneum, 1990.

Lech, Raymond B. *All the Drowned Sailors.* New York: Stein and Day, 1982.

Liddell Hart, B. H. *History of the Second World War.* New York: Putnam, 1971.

Macintyre, Donald. *The Battle for the Pacific.* New York: Norton, 1966.

Marks, R. Adrian. *Selected Speeches* (no date).

Matsuo, Kinoaki, and Kilsoo K. Haan, trans. *How Japan Plans to Win.* Boston: Little, Brown, 1942.

McCoy, Dr. Giles. Congressional statement. 14 September 1999.

McGuiggan, Robert. Congressional statement. 14 September 1999.

McVay, Capt. Charles. Personal log from life raft. 1945.

————Speech for the first survivors' reunion. 1960.

————Transcript of court-martial testimony. December 1945.

————Transcript of deposition. 15 November 1945.

————Transcript of deposition. 27 September 1945.

Moore, Katherine D. *Goodbye, Indy Maru: A Navy Wife Remembers.* Knoxville, Tenn.: Lori Publications, 1991.

Morison, Samuel Eliot. *Victory in the Pacific.* Boston: Little, Brown, 1960.

Murphy, Paul. Congressional statement. 14 September 1999.

Navy Department Press Release. "Narrative of the Circumstances of the Loss of the *Indianapolis.*" 23 February 1946.

Newcomb, Richard F. *Abandon Ship!: The Death of the USS* Indianapolis. New York: Henry Holt, 1958.

Philbrick, Nathaniel. *In the Heart of the Sea.* New York: Viking, 2000.

Pilling, Adm. Donald. Congressional statement. 14 September 1999.

Rosenfeld, Joseph. *Highway to Tokyo.* Boston: Little, Brown, 1943.

Salmaggi, Cesare, and Alfredo Pallavisini. *2,194 Days of War.* New York: Gallery Books, 1977.

Scott, Cmdr. Roger D. *Summary of Report on the Court-Martial of Captain Charles B. McVay III, USN, Commanding Officer, USS Indianapolis.* Washington: Government Printing Office, 1966.

———*Kimmel, Short, McVay: Case Studies in Executive Authority, Law and the Individual Rights of Military Commanders.* Washington: Government Printing Office, 1998.

Scott, Hunter. Congressional statement. 14 September 1999.

Senate Armed Forces Committee. Transcript of hearing. 14 September 1999.

Smith, Cozell. "For Peace of Mind." 1993.

Smith, Sen. Robert. Congressional statement. 27 October 1999.

———Congressional statement. 25 May 1999.

Solms, Mark. *The Neuropsychology of Dreams: A Clinico-Anatomical Study.* Mahwah, N.J.: Lawrence Erlbaum, 1997.

Springer, Victor G., and Joy P. Gold, eds. *Sharks in Question: The Smithsonian Answer Book.* Washington: Smithsonian Institute Press, 1989.

Stanton, Doug. *In Harm's Way.* New York: Henry Holt, 2001.

Toti, Cmdr. William J. "The Sinking of the *Indianapolis* and Responsibility of Command." *Proceedings Magazine,* October 1999.

Twible, Harlan. Congressional statement. 14 September 1999.

USS Indianapolis *(CA-35): Pride of the U.S. Navy, Final Tragedy of World War II.* Survivor Memorial Assn., 1992.

Von Doenhoff, Richard A. "ULTRA and the Sinking of the USS *Indianapolis.*" *Naval History Symposium,* 23 October 1993.

Zich, Arthur. *The Rising Sun.* New York: Time-Life Books, 1977.

Index

About the Author

PETE NELSON is the author of eighteen books of fiction and nonfiction and has written for numerous magazines. His most recent book, *That Others May Live* (Random House, 2000), tells the story of the air force's pararescue jumpers. He lives in Massachusetts with his wife and son.